Coaching Approaches Compared

This book provides an overview and comparative analysis of four major coaching approaches: Cognitive, Existential, Gestalt and Systems Psychodynamic coaching.

Throughout this book, the author offers an introduction to coaching and its benefits. He delves into the importance of building a strong coaching relationship and the fundamental skills and competencies needed, and then provides a comparison of the four different coaching models, approaches and philosophies along with their various tools and techniques. He then explores how each approach addresses different dimensions of leadership and human growth. Using identical fictional case studies, Fusco demonstrates how each method responds uniquely to the same leadership challenges, highlighting their distinct tools, interventions and underlying philosophies.

This book will appeal to both novice and experienced coaches, as well as leaders, HR professionals and those curious about the evolving field of coaching and how integrative approaches can support complex organisational development.

Tony Fusco, DPsych, is a chartered coaching psychologist with 20 years of experience in the field, specialising in the research and practice of group coaching for Authentic Leadership Development. He has a doctorate in coaching psychology from the University of London and is the author of *An Evidence-based Approach to Authentic Leadership Development* (Routledge, 2018).

Coaching Approaches Compared

A Practical Guide to Four Major Methodologies

Tony Fusco

Routledge
Taylor & Francis Group

LONDON AND NEW YORK

Designed cover image: Getty Images

First published 2026
by Routledge
4 Park Square, Milton Park, Abingdon, Oxon OX14 4RN

and by Routledge
605 Third Avenue, New York, NY 10158

Routledge is an imprint of the Taylor & Francis Group, an informa business

British Library Cataloguing-in-Publication Data
A catalogue record for this book is available from the British
Library

ISBN: 978-1-032-97541-2 (hbk)
ISBN: 978-1-032-97540-5 (pbk)
ISBN: 978-1-003-59421-5 (ebk)

DOI: 10.4324/9781003594215

Typeset in Times New Roman
by Apex CoVantage, LLC

Contents

Preface

As coaching practitioners, we may find ourselves drawn to a particular coaching methodology, sometimes dismissing others as somehow less effective or relevant. But when I first encountered the diverse world of coaching, I was struck by how each approach seemed to offer some valuable insights while also retaining distinct limitations.

Throughout my years working with leaders, teams and organisations, I've learned that the complex challenges facing today's leaders rarely conform to, or fully benefit from, a single theoretical framework. I have witnessed how different coaching approaches address different dimensions of the leadership experience. Some leaders respond powerfully to existential explorations of meaning and authenticity, while others benefit most from examining the unconscious dynamics influencing their organisations. Still others find transformation through present-moment awareness or by identifying and restructuring limiting beliefs and thought patterns.

And so, this book arose from my desire to provide an overview of four major coaching approaches – Existential, Systems Psychodynamic, Gestalt and Cognitive – and to demonstrate how they can be practised independently and integrated to create a more holistic and effective coaching practice. However, rather than arguing for the superiority of one approach over another, I've sought to illuminate the unique contributions of each and show how they can complement one another.

The individual case studies used in this book are fictional but represent composites of real situations. They illustrate how each coaching approach might address similar leadership challenges in distinct ways, offering the reader a practical understanding of these methodologies in action. I chose to replicate the team coaching case study across all four examples so readers could directly compare the different focus, direction and choice points of each of the methodologies within the same team context and challenge. The final sections on integrative coaching demonstrate how these approaches can be poetically woven together to address the multidimensional nature of leadership challenges.

This book is not intended as a technical manual for practising coaches, though I hope practitioners will find value in its comparative perspective. Rather, it aims to provide a clear and accessible overview of various coaching philosophies and their applications for anyone interested in how coaching can be applied to leadership

development, organisational effectiveness and personal growth. My hope is that
the book will encourage readers to approach coaching with an open mind, recognising that different approaches offer different windows into the human experience
and organisational life. Ultimately, by understanding the full spectrum of coaching
methodologies, we are able to select the most appropriate tools for specific contexts
while also appreciating the richness that an integrative perspective can bring.

Dr. Tony Fusco

2025

Introduction

Leadership has never been more challenging. In today's complex, rapidly changing world, leaders face unprecedented pressures to navigate uncertainty, foster innovation, build inclusive cultures and deliver sustainable results. So, it's no surprise that traditional approaches to leadership training and development often fall short in preparing individuals and teams for these multifaceted challenges.

Coaching has emerged as a powerful approach for developing the capacities leaders need to thrive in this environment. Unlike traditional training, coaching creates a reflective space where leaders can examine their assumptions, expand their perspectives and develop new ways of thinking and being. In this field, coaching encompasses several diverse approaches, each with its own distinct philosophical foundations, methodologies and focus.

This book examines four main coaching approaches – Existential, Systems Psychodynamic, Gestalt and Cognitive – that offer complementary perspectives on leadership development, with each approach illuminating different dimensions of individual and organisational life. These approaches include the following:

- *Existential Coaching* – addresses fundamental questions of meaning, purpose, authenticity and choice. It helps leaders connect with what truly matters and make conscious choices aligned with their values amidst the pressures of organisational life.
- *Systems Psychodynamic Coaching* – explores how unconscious processes influence behaviour in organisations. It reveals hidden patterns, anxieties and defences that shape leadership and team dynamics beyond rational awareness.
- *Gestalt Coaching* – focuses on present-moment awareness and authentic contact. It helps leaders develop greater presence, integrate polarised aspects of experience and recognise patterns as they emerge in real time.
- *Cognitive Coaching* – examines thinking patterns that influence perception, decision-making and behaviour. It helps leaders recognise and refine their mental models to enhance their effectiveness and adaptability.

While each approach offers its own valuable insights, real-world leadership challenges rarely fit neatly within a single framework. The most effective coaching

DOI: 10.4324/9781003594215-1

often integrates multiple perspectives to address the full spectrum of leadership development, and so the final section of this book explores how these approaches can be woven together into a comprehensive and integrative coaching approach.

Throughout this book, case studies illustrate how each approach might work with similar leadership challenges. These fictional scenarios demonstrate the distinct contributions each methodology makes while highlighting opportunities for integration. The book examines these approaches in both individual and team contexts, recognising that leadership and its development often happen at multiple levels simultaneously.

Who Will Benefit from Reading This Book?

A broad range of professionals might benefit from the unique approach this book takes to exploring the field of coaching. These may include:

I. Coaching Practitioners – will gain a comparative understanding of four major coaching approaches and practical insights for integrating them. While novice coaches will find a comprehensive introduction to diverse methodologies, more experienced practitioners may also discover new perspectives to enhance their existing practice. The case studies provide valuable examples of how various approaches can address similar challenges.

II. Leaders and Executives – will develop a deeper understanding of coaching as a leadership development tool. By recognising the different dimensions addressed by various coaching approaches, leaders can make more informed choices about their own development and better support the growth of those they lead.

III. HR and Organisational Development Professionals – will find this book valuable when selecting coaching interventions for their own organisations. Understanding the strengths and applications of different approaches can enable more strategic matching of coaching methodologies to specific leadership and organisational challenges.

IV. Team Leaders and Facilitators – will benefit from the chapters on team coaching, which illuminate how different approaches can enhance team functioning and collaboration. The team case studies demonstrate how various methodologies address common team dynamics and challenges.

V. Leadership Educators – can use this book to broaden their conceptual frameworks and incorporate diverse perspectives into leadership development programmes. The comparative approach may also provide a foundation for more comprehensive curriculum design.

VI. Psychology and Business Students – will find this book a practical bridge between psychological theories and their applications in organisational and leadership development.

VII. Anyone Interested in Personal Development – will discover frameworks for understanding their own individual patterns, choices and relationships. While focused on organisational applications, the approaches described in this book also offer insights relevant to personal growth and self-awareness more broadly.

The intention is not to advocate for any single coaching approach but to illuminate the unique contributions each makes to our understanding of individual, leadership and organisational development. The aim is that by appreciating the full spectrum of coaching methodologies, we can develop more nuanced and effective approaches to the complex challenges leaders and organisations increasingly face.

The journey through these pages invites you to expand your perspective on coaching and leadership development. Whether you're a seasoned coach, an experienced leader or simply curious about different approaches to human development in organisational contexts, I hope this exploration will enrich your understanding and practice.

Part 1

Four Major Approaches to Coaching

Chapter 1

Existential Coaching

Existential coaching evolved from existential philosophy, which emerged in the 19th and 20th centuries through the works of philosophers like Søren Kierkegaard (1813–1855), Friedrich Nietzsche (1844–1900), Martin Heidegger (1889–1976) and Jean-Paul Sartre (1905–1980). These thinkers explored questions about the nature of existence, human freedom, the search for meaning and the challenges of confronting life's uncertainties.

Existential psychology was then developed by figures such as Rollo May (1909–1994), Viktor Frankl (1905–1997) and Irvin Yalom (1931–), who applied existential philosophy to understanding human psychological experiences, emphasising personal responsibility, choice and the search for meaning in life.

In the coaching context, existential coaching began to emerge as a response to the limitations of more traditional coaching approaches that focused primarily on goals, behaviours and performance outcomes. Existential coaching seeks to address deeper existential concerns and existential crises that individuals may face in their lives and careers.

Key Principles and Aims

Existential coaching is based on several fundamental principles. Some of them are as follows:

Freedom and responsibility: We are free to make choices but must also take responsibility for these choices and their consequences. Existential coaches help clients recognise their freedom and the responsibilities that come with it.

Authenticity: Living in alignment with one's true values and nature rather than conforming to external expectations. Existential coaches help clients discover what authenticity means for them personally.

Meaning and purpose: Finding or creating meaning in life is essential for psychological well-being. Existential coaches help clients explore what gives their lives meaning.

DOI: 10.4324/9781003594215-3

Acceptance of uncertainty and mortality: Acknowledging that life is tempo-rary and uncertain can lead to a more authentic and meaningful existence. Coaches help clients face existential anxieties about death, isolation and meaninglessness.

An existential coaching relationship typically involves:

- Deep exploration of the client's worldview, values and beliefs
- Examination of how the client creates meaning in their life
- Exploration of authentic choices versus choices made to please others
- Confronting existential givens (mortality, freedom, isolation, meaninglessness)
- Developing greater self-awareness and personal responsibility
- Creating a more authentic and meaningful path through life and work

Unlike some forms of coaching that focus on specific outcomes or goals, existen-tial coaching is more process-oriented. The coach creates a reflective space where clients can explore fundamental questions about their existence and make choices that align with their authentic selves. Therefore, it can be a particularly powerful approach for people experiencing major life transitions, questioning their purpose or direction, feeling trapped in inauthentic life patterns, facing significant deci-sions, dealing with loss, illness or other reminders of mortality or generally seeking greater meaning and authenticity in their lives.

In sum, existential coaching creates a space for individuals to confront life's fundamental questions and develop a more authentic relationship with themselves and their existence. While cognitive-behavioural coaching might focus on chang-ing thought patterns to achieve goals, for example and solution-focused coaching might emphasise concrete actions towards specific outcomes, existential coaching delves into the deeper questions of what makes those goals worthwhile in the first place. It's less about "how to succeed" and more about "what success truly means for you."

Existential Coaching: A Deeper Exploration

Let's expand on each of the key principles that form the foundation of existential coaching.

Freedom and Responsibility

In existential philosophy, freedom is an ontological condition of being human. We are "condemned to freedom," as Sartre put it, meaning we cannot escape the neces-sity of choosing. Even choosing not to choose is itself a choice.

Existential coaching helps clients recognise the extent of their freedom and the ways they might be denying it. Many people feel trapped by circumstances, but an existential approach reveals how we often create these traps ourselves through our interpretations and choices. The coach might ask questions such as "What choices are you avoiding making?" or "How are you pretending to be a victim when you actually have agency?" These questions can be deeply uncomfortable because they confront the client with their ultimate self-responsibility.

Responsibility in this context isn't about blame but about authorship of one's life. When clients embrace this responsibility, they often experience both anxiety (from the weight of choice) and liberation (from the possibility of change). An effective existential coach will create a safe space to explore this tension. For example, a client might say, "I have to stay in this job I hate because I need the money." An existential coach might gently challenge this by exploring what values the client is prioritising (security over fulfilment) and whether this is a conscious, authentic choice or an unexamined assumption.

Authenticity

Authenticity is perhaps the central value in existential coaching. It refers to living in accordance with one's true self rather than conforming to external expectations or falling into what Heidegger called "das Man" – the anonymous "they" who dictate social norms.

Existential coaches help clients distinguish between their authentic desires and those they've absorbed from family, culture or society. This involves examining the "scripts" we follow without questioning. This process often involves identifying where the client feels most like "themselves" versus where they feel they're playing a role, exploring feelings of emptiness or meaninglessness as potential signals of inauthenticity, examining the fear of disappointing others and how it limits authentic expression, and helping clients recognise and overcome "bad faith" – Sartre's term for the self-deception that this can all lead to.

For instance, a client might have pursued a prestigious career to please their parents but feels empty despite their success. An existential coach would help them explore what truly matters to them, separate from external validation.

Existential authenticity doesn't mean acting on every impulse but rather making choices that align with one's deeply held values and true nature. It often requires courage, as authentic choices may not always be socially rewarded or understood by others.

Meaning and Purpose

Viktor Frankl's work on logotherapy emphasises that the primary human motivation is not pleasure or power but the search for meaning. Existential coaching builds on this insight by helping clients discover or create meaning in their lives.

Unlike some philosophical approaches that view the universe as inherently meaningless, existential coaching takes the perspective that although objective meaning may be lacking, subjective meaning is both possible and essential for human flourishing.

The coach might help clients, therefore, explore what activities give them a sense of purpose or flow, what values they want their lives to embody, how they can contribute to something larger than themselves and how suffering or challenges can be transformed through the meaning they assign to them. Frankl observed that people can endure almost any "how" if they have a strong enough "why." Existential coaching helps clients find their "why" – not by prescribing it, but by helping them uncover it within themselves.

This might involve exercises like imagining one's eulogy, identifying peak experiences or contemplating what one would regret not doing if they knew their time was limited. These thought experiments can reveal what truly matters to the client beneath surface-level goals.

Acceptance of Uncertainty and Mortality

Existential philosophy recognises several "givens" of human existence: death, freedom, isolation and meaninglessness. Rather than avoiding these uncomfortable truths, existential coaching encourages clients to face them directly.

Awareness of mortality, in particular, can transform how we live. When clients acknowledge that their time is finite, priorities often shift dramatically. The coach might ask, "If you knew you had only a year to live, what would change about how you're living now?" This isn't meant to be morbid but to clarify what truly matters to the client.

Uncertainty is another existential given. We cannot predict the future or control all outcomes, yet many people expend enormous energy trying to eliminate uncertainty from their lives. Existential coaching helps clients develop comfort with not knowing and find freedom within such uncertainty. This principle also addresses existential anxiety – the unease that comes from facing life's fundamental questions. Rather than pathologising this anxiety or trying to eliminate it, existential coaches see it as a natural response to human existence and potentially a catalyst for growth. For example, a client feeling anxiety about a major life decision might be helped to see this anxiety not as something to avoid but as a sign they're engaging with important questions. The coach might help them distinguish between neurotic anxiety (based on irrational fears) and existential anxiety (based on genuine life challenges).

Developing Greater Self-Awareness and Personal Responsibility

Existential coaching places tremendous emphasis on self-awareness as the foundation for authentic living. This involves helping clients recognise their patterns, biases, defences and blind spots. The existential coach creates conditions where clients see themselves and their situations with unusual clarity, moments when habitual ways of thinking are often disrupted.

This development of self-awareness might include the following:

- Examining how past experiences shape current perspectives
- Recognising patterns in relationships and life choices
- Exploring contradictions between stated values and actual behaviours
- Identifying defence mechanisms that prevent authentic engagement

Personal responsibility builds on this self-awareness. As clients become more aware of their patterns, they also become more capable of making different choices. The existential coach emphasises that while we cannot control all circumstances, we can always control our response to those circumstances. This isn't about positive thinking or denial of real constraints but about finding the space for choice even in difficult situations. As Frankl noted from his experience in concentration camps, "Everything can be taken from a man but one thing: the last of the human freedoms – to choose one's attitude in any given set of circumstances."

Creating a More Authentic and Meaningful Path Forward

The culmination of existential coaching is helping clients craft lives that have personal meaning and reflect their authentic values. This isn't about following a predetermined plan but about living with greater awareness and intentionality. To this end, the coach might help clients make decisions based on their authentic values rather than just external pressures; build courage to face the anxiety that comes with these authentic choices and find purpose through a contribution to others or causes larger than themselves.

Unlike coaching approaches focused primarily on achievement, existential coaching measures success by the quality of engagement with life rather than specific outcomes. A client may not achieve every external goal, but they may still consider the coaching successful if they are living with greater authenticity and meaning. For example, a client might enter coaching wanting a promotion but discover through the process that what they really value is creative expression. Success might then involve finding ways to incorporate creativity into their current role or transitioning to a different career altogether.

The existential coach doesn't direct this process but serves as a travelling companion, helping clients discover their own path by asking powerful questions and creating space for deep reflection. Throughout this journey, the relationship between coach and client models the authentic engagement that the client is working to develop in their broader life – characterised by presence, honesty and mutual respect for individual freedom and choice.

Applying Existential Coaching in the Workplace

Existential coaching can be remarkably effective in workplace settings, offering profound benefits for both individuals and organisations. When applied thoughtfully, this philosophical approach can help address deeper questions of meaning, purpose and authenticity that conventional workplace coaching might overlook.

Finding Meaning in Work

Many people struggle with the feeling that their work lacks significance. Existential coaching helps employees explore how their work may or may not connect to their values and may or may not contribute to something more meaningful.

For example, a marketing professional might discover deeper meaning by understanding how their work helps customers find solutions to real problems. Instead of focusing only on metrics and targets, they might reframe their work in terms of human connection and service. This shift in perspective can transform routine tasks into a more purposeful activity. An existential coach might ask questions like "Beyond earning a living, what purpose does your work serve?" or "What aspects of your work align most closely with what matters to you?" These questions invite employees to discover or create meaning even in seemingly meaningless roles.

Embracing Workplace Freedom and Responsibility

Even when employees feel constrained by workplace structures and rules, existential coaching can help them recognise the freedom they do have – to choose their attitude, to take initiative within constraints and to shape their experience. The approach promotes taking responsibility rather than blaming external factors for workplace challenges. Instead of seeing themselves as victims of circumstance, employees learn to ask: "Given these constraints, what choices remain available to me?"

For instance, someone feeling trapped in a rigid corporate structure might work with a coach to identify "choice points" throughout their day where they actually have more autonomy than they realised. This might include how they approach conversations, what projects they volunteer for, how they manage their energy or even how they choose to interact with colleagues.

Developing Workplace Authenticity

Many professionals find that their careers require them to wear a "work mask" that differs from their authentic self. While some professional boundaries are necessary, extreme disconnection between one's work persona and one's true self can lead to disengagement or even alienation.

Existential coaching can help bridge this gap by exploring questions like "Where do you feel most authentic at work?" and "What aspects of yourself do you feel you need to hide, and what would happen if you expressed them more openly?" For example, a naturally creative person in a highly structured role might work with a coach to find appropriate outlets for their creativity within their current position, rather than suppressing this essential aspect of themselves.

Confronting Career Anxiety and Uncertainty

Contemporary career paths are increasingly non-linear and unpredictable. Existential coaching can help professionals navigate this uncertainty by developing comfort with not knowing all the answers and finding meaning in the journey itself. For example, a coach might help someone anxious about their career trajectory examine the roots of their anxiety and distinguish between productive concern and paralysing worry. This might involve exploring questions like "What would it mean to embrace career uncertainty rather than fear it?" or "How might this uncertainty actually create possibilities you haven't considered?"

Authentic Leadership Development

Leaders who struggle with balancing organisational demands and authentic self-expression can use existential coaching to help them identify and live their values more consistently, and lead through genuine presence rather than performing an expected leadership role.

A coach might help a leader explore questions like "What kind of leader do you truly want to be, beyond what management books prescribe?" or "Where do your personal values align or conflict with organisational expectations, and how can you navigate this tension authentically?" The result is often leadership that feels more natural and sustainable, inspiring greater trust from team members who sense the leader's authenticity.

Leaders also have significant influence over whether their own team members experience work as meaningful. Existential coaching can help leaders consider how they can foster environments where people connect their work to a greater purpose. This might involve helping leaders articulate the "why" behind tasks and projects, not just the "what" and "how"; create space for team members to express their values and connect them to work; recognise and celebrate meaningful contributions beyond measurable outcomes; or design roles that align with individuals' sources of meaning when possible.

In addition, during periods of organisational change, existential coaching can help leaders maintain perspective and guide their teams through uncertainty. Rather than pretending to have all of the answers, leaders learn to acknowledge the uncertainty while providing stability through consistent values and purpose. An existential coach might help leaders explore questions such as "What remains constant even as everything changes?" or "How can you help your team find meaning in this transitional period?"

Existential coaching approaches can also be applied to team development, helping teams move beyond superficial interactions to more meaningful collaboration. Team exercises might explore questions like:

- "What values do we share as a team, and how do they show up in our work?"
- "How can we create space for each person to bring their authentic self to our collaboration?"

- "How do our team dynamics support or hinder authentic expression?"
- "What gives our work together meaning beyond just completing tasks?"
- "How do we manage uncertainly, ambiguity and change?"

Teams frequently face difficult choices with no clear "right" answer. In these instances, existential coaching can help them develop frameworks for decision-making based on shared values rather than just metrics. For example, a product team deciding between different features might be guided to consider not just which option would drive more sales but also which aligns better with their values around user experience, accessibility or sustainability.

In the workplace, existential coaching isn't about philosophical discussions detached from practical realities. Rather, it's about connecting day-to-day work to deeper human needs for meaning, authenticity and purpose – ultimately creating more engaged employees, more effective leaders and more vibrant organisations. It represents a philosophical, introspective approach to coaching that goes beyond traditional goal-setting and behaviour change. By exploring existential themes that promote self-awareness, authenticity and personal responsibility, existential coaching empowers individuals to live more meaningful, purposeful lives aligned with their deepest values and aspirations. Its effectiveness lies in its ability to support clients in navigating life's complexities with courage, resilience and clarity of purpose.

Practical Starting Points

To start applying elements of Existential Coaching in the workplace, consider some of the following:

1. Start with meaning exploration: Begin coaching conversations by helping employees explore what brings meaning to their work. Ask questions such as "What aspects of your work feel most meaningful to you?" or "When do you feel most aligned with your purpose here?" This helps connect daily tasks to deeper values and motivations.
2. Embrace choice awareness: Help individuals recognise the choices they make daily, even in constrained workplace environments. Encourage them to recognise where they have agency and how their choices shape their professional experience. This shifts the perspective from "I have to" to "I choose to."
3. Normalise existential anxiety: Create space for discussions about workplace uncertainty and change. Help employees understand that anxiety about professional identity, direction and impact is normal and can be a catalyst for growth rather than something to suppress.
4. Incorporate values clarification exercises: Guide employees in articulating their core values and examining how these align with their current role and organisation. This creates a foundation for making authentic career decisions and finding greater congruence between personal values and work life.

5. Practise radical responsibility: Encourage individuals to take ownership of their workplace experience rather than defaulting to victimhood or blame. Help them recognise how they co-create their professional reality and can actively shape their relationships and environment.

6. Explore work-life finitude: Facilitate reflections on the limited nature of professional time and energy. Questions like "If you had only one year left in your career, how would you spend it?" can help prioritise what truly matters and reduce fixation on trivial workplace concerns.

7. Create authentic dialogue spaces: Establish coaching conversations as zones where professional personas can be temporarily set aside. Encourage genuine expression of doubts, fears and aspirations without judgement, allowing individuals to access deeper insights about their work experience and future direction.

Each of these suggestions serves as an entry point for existential themes in workplace coaching without requiring extensive philosophical background. As trust develops, deeper existential explorations around choice, responsibility, meaning and purpose can naturally emerge in professionally relevant ways.

Further Reading

Cox, E., Bachkirova, T., & Clutterbuck, D. (Eds.). (2018). *The complete handbook of coaching* (3rd ed.). Sage Publications. [Chapters on existential coaching approaches].

Diamond, J. (2020). *Existential coaching skills: The handbook for practitioners*. Routledge.

Krum, A. K. (2018). *The existential leader: An authentic approach to leadership for challenging times*. Routledge.

Langdridge, D. (2013). *Existential counselling and psychotherapy*. Sage Publications.

Nanda, J. (2019). *Mindful existential coaching: A holistic approach to executive development*. Palgrave Macmillan.

Passmore, J., & Tee, D. (2021). *Coaching in three dimensions: Meeting the challenges of a complex world*. Routledge.

Spinelli, E. (2014). *Being in the world: Existential perspectives on coaching*. Routledge.

Spinelli, E. (2015). Practicing existential coaching. In S. Palmer & A. Whybrow (Eds.), *Handbook of coaching psychology: A guide for practitioners* (2nd ed., pp. 198–212). Routledge.

Van Deurzen, E. (2012). *Existential counselling & psychotherapy in practice* (3rd ed.). Sage Publications.

Van Deurzen, E., & Hanaway, M. (Eds.). (2018). *Existential perspectives on coaching*. Palgrave Macmillan.

Yalom, I. D. (2020). *Existential psychotherapy* (2nd ed.). Basic Books.

Chapter 2

Systems Psychodynamic Coaching

Systems psychodynamic coaching evolved from the field of organisational psychology and psychoanalysis. It draws on the works of key theorists such as Wilfred Bion (1897–1979), Melanie Klein (1882–1960) and Donald Winnicott (1896–1971) in psychoanalysis, as well as Kurt Lewin (1890–1947) and his work in group dynamics and organisational behaviour.

In the mid-20th century, researchers and practitioners began to explore how unconscious processes and group dynamics impact organisational behaviour and performance. The Tavistock Institute in London played a significant role in developing systems psychodynamic theory and practice, particularly through its application in organisational consulting and coaching. Systems psychodynamic coaching applies all of the insights gained from these approaches to help individuals and organisations understand and address complex interpersonal and systemic issues that affect performance, collaboration and leadership effectiveness.

It is an approach to coaching that integrates systems thinking with psychodynamic concepts to understand both the conscious and unconscious factors influencing workplace behaviour and organisational dynamics. Unlike other approaches that may focus more on visible behaviours or cognitive processes, systems psychodynamic coaching examines the deeper psychological and systemic forces at play beneath the surface. The approach views human behaviour in organisations as determined not only by conscious goals and strategies but also by unconscious motives, fantasies and anxieties. It recognises that much of organisational life happens "below the surface" and that sustainable change requires addressing these deeper dynamics rather than merely focusing on surface symptoms.

Systems Psychodynamics' fundamental philosophy recognises that organisations are not merely rational entities but also emotional arenas where unconscious processes significantly influence behaviour. All of these unconscious dynamics, such as anxiety, defence mechanisms, projection and transference, operate at individual, group and organisational levels.

DOI: 10.4324/9781003594215-4

Key Principles and Aims

A key principle is that systems psychodynamic coaching sees organisations as containers for anxiety – as structures that help people manage the uncertainties and emotional challenges of work. When this containing function works well, anxiety is held at manageable levels, allowing productive work. When it fails, anxiety may overwhelm individuals or groups, leading to dysfunctional behaviours.

Coaches working from this perspective help clients understand how organisational structures and processes serve psychological functions beyond their stated practical purposes. For example, excessive paperwork might ostensibly exist for accountability, but psychologically function to create an illusion of control in uncertain times. A coach might help an executive recognise how their insistence on detailed reporting is not just about information gathering but also serving to manage their anxiety about delegating authority.

Systems Psychodynamic Coaching: A Deeper Exploration

Social Defences Against Anxiety

Organisations and groups have a tendency to develop collective social defence mechanisms, that is to protect members from the anxieties inherent in their work. Over time, these defences can become embedded in organisational structures, processes and culture, often at the cost of effective performance. Systems psychodynamic coaches can help clients identify these social defences in their own organisations and understand their psychological purposes. This recognition can enable the development of more conscious and adaptive ways of managing anxiety without compromising the *primary task*. For instance, a coach might help a leadership team recognise how their avoidance of conflict in meetings serves as a social defence against the anxiety of disagreement, but at the cost of making effective decisions. This awareness could lead to developing more constructive approaches to conflict that acknowledge the underlying anxiety while still allowing necessary tensions to be worked on.

The Primary Task and Anti-Task

The systems-psychodynamic approach emphasises the concept of the "primary task" – the core purpose that justifies an organisation's existence. Anxiety can often lead organisations to drift from their primary task towards "anti-task" behaviours that appear to serve the organisational mission but actually just defend against work-related anxieties. For example, a school's primary task is educating students, but it might drift towards excessive testing or paperwork that creates the illusion of educational activity while actually defending against the anxiety of engaging with the messy, unpredictable process of true learning. Or perhaps, a non-profit organisation has drifted from its mission of community service towards an excessive focus on fundraising events. While necessary, fundraising has become an anti-task behaviour that defends against the anxiety of engaging directly with difficult community issues. The systems psychodynamic coach can help these clients distinguish between the activities that genuinely serve their primary tasks and those that function as anti-task behaviours. This brings a clarity and recognition that can help the leadership team rebalance priorities in a way that allows them to refocus their energy on their organisation's core purpose rather than on defensive routines.

Role and Authority

Systems psychodynamic coaching also pays attention to how people take up their roles within organisations. It distinguishes between the "normative" role (formal job description and expectations) and the "phenomenological" role (how the person actually experiences and performs the role). Gaps and conflicts between these aspects of the role often create tension that affects performance and well-being. So, coaches might help clients explore these different dimensions of their roles and help them work towards greater and healthier integration. This coaching approach also examines how authority is authorised and exercised within organisations. It recognises that formal authority must be complemented by psychological authority for effective leadership. A coach might help a newly promoted manager who is struggling to assert authority understand how their internal experience of the role (e.g. feeling like an impostor) conflicts with the formal expectations of that role. This exploration could address unconscious beliefs about authority stemming from the leader's personal history and/or current organisational dynamics that prevent them from fully taking up their role.

Boundaries

Psychological, task, time, territory and role boundaries are essential for containing anxiety and enabling productive work. Systems psychodynamic coaching examines how boundaries are established, maintained and violated in organisations. Coaches can help clients recognise when boundaries are too rigid (leading to silos and inflexibility) or too permeable (creating confusion and anxiety). They can explore how boundary issues relate to deeper anxieties about separation, inclusion/exclusion and identity. For example, a coach might help a team leader understand how unclear boundaries between their department and others create anxiety and territorial conflicts. This might reveal underlying fears about loss of identity or control that need to be addressed for better collaboration. Systems psychodynamic coaching usually involves deep exploration of the client's organisational experiences, going beyond surface presentations to understand the underlying dynamics at play within the system they are embedded within.

Applying Systems Psychodynamic Coaching in the Workplace

Systems psychodynamic coaching can bring unique insights to workplace challenges by examining the deeper currents beneath surface behaviours. It can be particularly valuable in workplace settings where emotional and political undercurrents significantly influence behaviour and performance. Here's how this approach can be applied to address common workplace situations:

Leadership Development

For individual leaders, systems psychodynamic coaching can help with:

- Understanding how personal history influences leadership style and responses to authority
- Recognising projection processes that shape how others perceive and respond to them
- Identifying unconscious anxieties that drive reactive behaviours or decisions
- Taking up authority more effectively by understanding unconscious barriers
- Managing boundaries between different aspects of their professional and personal life

Many leaders struggle with fully taking up their authority, either overcompensating with excessive control or avoiding decisive action. Systems psychodynamic coaching can help leaders understand these psychological dimensions of authority relations. A coach might help a leader explore how their personal history with authority figures (parents, teachers, early bosses) shapes their current relationship with their own authority. For instance, a leader who had a domineering parent might unconsciously associate authoritative action with abuse of power, leading to an overly consultative style that reflects their anxiety about authority rather than being a genuine commitment to collaboration. The coach creates space for the leader to distinguish between these internalised authority figures and their own authentic approach to power, helping them develop authority that's neither abdicating nor authoritarian but grounded in their role, purpose and values.

Leaders also serve as containers for organisational anxiety, helping the system manage uncertainty and stress at sustainable levels. Systems psychodynamic coaching helps leaders develop this containing function. A coach might help a CEO recognise how their anxious reactions to market pressures cascade through the organisation, amplifying stress at every level. By developing greater capacity to hold their own anxiety rather than transmitting it, the leader can create a more thoughtful, less reactive organisational culture. The coach might work with the leader on developing "negative capability" – the ability to stay present with uncertainty without prematurely rushing to action. This capacity helps the leader distinguish between situations requiring immediate response and those benefiting from reflective space, thus preventing anxiety-driven decisions.

Team Development

For teams, systems psychodynamic coaching approaches can support the:

- Uncovering of unconscious group dynamics that might be undermining performance
- Understanding how the team functions as a social system with formal and informal roles
- Recognising scapegoating and other projection processes within the team
- Addressing anxiety-driven behaviours that hinder collaboration or decision-making
- Developing the team's capacity to contain and work with difficult emotions
- Clarifying boundaries and authority relations within the team

Teams often develop collective defences against anxiety that hinder performance while providing psychological comfort. Systems psychodynamic coaching helps teams recognise and modify these defences when they become dysfunctional. For example, a coach might help a product development team recognise how their lengthy, detailed planning processes not just serve practical purposes but also defend against the anxiety of uncertainty inherent in innovation. By acknowledging this anxiety directly, the team might develop more appropriate ways to manage it without sacrificing agility. Similarly, a team that relies on the same person to challenge ideas might recognise this as a defence against the anxiety of conflict – by containing disagreement in one role, others can maintain harmonious relationships. This awareness could lead to developing more distributed responsibility for constructive challenge.

Organisational Change

In organisational change contexts, systems psychodynamic coaching can help leaders:

- Understand resistance to change as a complex psychological phenomenon
- Recognise how change threatens identity and triggers loss and grief responses
- Address the anxiety that change inevitably produces rather than trying to eliminate it
- Design change processes that provide adequate psychological containment
- Work with the emotional symbolic dimensions of change, as well as practical aspects

For example, a coach might help a leader implementing a major restructuring understand that employee resistance stems not just from fear of job loss but also from grief about losing a valued organisational identity and relationships. This understanding could lead to change strategies that acknowledge these losses and create transitional spaces for processing them. This in-depth understanding allows for change strategies that address the psychological dimension of transformation, not just its practical aspects, leading to more sustainable change with less psychological cost.

Overall, the systems-psychodynamic approach can help an organisation start to notice and tune into emotional undercurrents that exist within their organisational systems. They can help them pay attention to repetitive patterns in the organisation – problems that persist and resist solution, conflicts that recur in different forms or roles that seem to remain constant even with personnel changes – all things which often indicate deeper systemic dynamics. This form of coaching is especially effective in helping to identify the unconscious functions in the system that these persistent patterns ultimately serve.

However, systems psychodynamic coaching doesn't offer quick fixes for such organisational challenges. Instead, it provides a depth of understanding that can lead to more sustainable solutions by addressing root causes rather than symptoms. By recognising and working with the unconscious and systemic dynamics that influence behaviour, this approach helps create organisations where both task accomplishment and psychological well-being are possible.

Organisational Politics and Power Dynamics

Workplace politics often represent unconscious dynamics surrounding authority, identity and anxiety. Systems psychodynamic coaching can help professionals understand these dynamics rather than simply being victimised by them or cynically playing the game. For example, a department head experiencing persistent conflicts with peers might work with a coach to understand how departmental boundaries have become battlegrounds for deeper organisational anxieties about resource scarcity or status. Rather than seeing these conflicts as merely interpersonal, the coach helps the client explore how they might be manifestations of systemic tensions.

This approach doesn't eliminate politics but transforms engagement with political dynamics from unconscious participation to conscious navigation, addressing underlying anxieties rather than merely their symptomatic expressions. For instance, a company that repeatedly hires visionary leaders who initially inspire enthusiasm but ultimately leave in frustration might work with a coach to understand this as a systemic pattern rather than a series of unfortunate accidents. The coach might help executives explore how this cycle serves as a social defence – allowing the organisation to simultaneously maintain the fantasy of transformation while actually protecting itself from the anxiety of real change. By recognising these deeper dynamics, the organisation can address the underlying anxieties rather than unconsciously repeating the pattern with each new leader.

Systems psychodynamic coaching offers an in-depth perspective on workplace challenges that complements more surface-focused approaches. By recognising and working with the unconscious and systemic dynamics that influence behaviour, this approach enables more sustainable change that addresses root causes rather than symptoms. While it requires comfort with complexity and ambiguity, it offers rich insights that can transform individual performance and organisational functioning at fundamental levels.

Practical Starting Points

To start applying Systems Psychodynamic Coaching techniques in the workplace, consider these initial steps:

1. Map the organisational system: Begin by helping colleagues or clients visualise their place within the larger organisational system. Have them draw or describe the formal and informal power structures, relationships and dynamics that shape their work environment. This creates awareness of how individual challenges may be expressions of larger systemic patterns.
2. Explore role boundaries: Guide employees in examining how they take up their professional roles. Help them distinguish between their formal role (as defined by job descriptions), the role as they perceive it and the role as others experience it. This illuminates unconscious role dynamics and boundary issues that may be creating workplace tension.
3. Identify parallel processes: Teach others to recognise when dynamics in one part of the system are mirrored elsewhere. For example, if a manager feels micromanaged by their boss, explore how they might unconsciously replicate this pattern with their team. This awareness helps break unconscious systemic patterns.
4. Work with projections: Help individuals recognise when they're projecting unacknowledged feelings or attributes onto colleagues or departments. Create a safe space to explore questions such as "What qualities do you find most frustrating in your difficult colleague, and how might these relate to disowned aspects of yourself?"
5. Surface-hidden group anxieties: Facilitate conversations about unspoken collective fears that may be driving dysfunctional workplace behaviours. Help leaders recognise how organisational defences against anxiety (like excessive bureaucracy or blame cultures) may be undermining performance and well-being.
6. Explore authority relations: Guide leaders in examining their relationship patterns with authority figures. Help them connect current authority dynamics with formative experiences and identify how unconscious patterns might be influencing their leadership style or responses to management.
7. Attend to relationships as data: Use the here-and-now dynamics between individuals as valuable information about wider organisational patterns. When tensions, expectations or dependencies emerge, explore how these might mirror dynamics in the workplace system.

These entry points help introduce systems psychodynamic thinking in accessible ways, creating foundations for deeper explorations of unconscious organisational life, containment, primary task and group-level defences as awareness develops.

Further Reading

Brunning, H. (2006). *Executive coaching: Systems-psychodynamic perspective*. Karnac Books.

Czander, W. M. (2012). *The psychodynamics of work and organizations: Theory and application*. Guilford Press.

De Haan, E. (2021). *The Tavistock tradition for leadership and organizational coaching*. Routledge.

Diamond, M. A. (2017). *Discovering organizational identity: Dynamics of relational attachment*. University of Missouri Press.

Eisold, K. (2012). *Psychoanalytic perspectives on organizational consulting: The unconscious side of organizational life*. Lexington Books.

French, R., & Simpson, P. (2015). *Attention, cooperation, purpose: An approach to working in groups using insights from Wilfred Bion*. Routledge.

Huffington, C., Armstrong, D., Halton, W., Hoyle, L., & Pooley, J. (Eds.). (2018). *Working below the surface: The emotional life of contemporary organizations*. Routledge.

Kets de Vries, M. F. R. (2014). *Mindful leadership coaching: Journeys into the interior*. Palgrave Macmillan.

Long, S. (Ed.). (2013). *Socioanalytic methods: Discovering the hidden in organisations and social systems*. Routledge.

Newton, J., Long, S., & Sievers, B. (Eds.). (2015). *Coaching in depth: The organizational role analysis approach*. Routledge.

Obholzer, A., & Roberts, V. Z. (Eds.). (2019). *The unconscious at work: A Tavistock approach to making sense of organizational life* (2nd ed.). Routledge.

Sher, M. (2013). *The dynamics of change: Tavistock approaches to improving social systems*. Routledge.

Stapley, L. F. (2006). *Individuals, groups, and organizations beneath the surface: An introduction*. Routledge.

Chapter 3

Gestalt Coaching

Gestalt coaching represents a powerful and holistic approach to professional development that emphasises awareness, personal responsibility and present-moment experience as catalysts for meaningful change. The German word "Gestalt" roughly translates to "whole," "pattern" or "form," reflecting the approach's focus on perceiving complete patterns rather than isolated fragments. Rooted in Gestalt psychology, developed by Fritz Perls (1893–1970) in the mid-20th century, this coaching methodology has evolved into a sophisticated framework particularly well-suited to navigating the complexities of modern organisational life. Unlike more directive coaching approaches that focus primarily on specific behaviours or outcomes, Gestalt coaching addresses the whole person – their thoughts, emotions, physical sensations and relational patterns – operating from the fundamental principle that sustainable change emerges from heightened awareness rather than prescriptive advice or techniques. At its core, Gestalt coaching is guided by the paradoxical theory of change, which suggests that transformation occurs not when individuals strive to become something they are not, but rather when they fully acknowledge and accept who they are in the present moment.

The distinctive power of Gestalt coaching lies in its experiential nature and phenomenological approach. Rather than analysing past events or future possibilities from an intellectual distance, Gestalt coaches invite clients to become fully present to their immediate experience, noticing what emerges in the "here and now" of the coaching relationship. Through skilled observation and powerful feedback, coaches help clients identify unrecognised patterns, unfinished business and contact boundaries that may be limiting their effectiveness or satisfaction in professional contexts. Gestalt interventions often involve creative experiments that bring subconscious patterns into conscious awareness, allowing clients to recognise how they may be interrupting their natural cycle of experience – whether through what Gestalt terms projection, introjection, retroflection, deflection or confluence. Perhaps more than any other coaching methodology, the Gestalt coach serves not as an expert but as a collaborative partner who supports clients in expanding their field of awareness and experimenting with new ways of being and doing.

DOI: 10.4324/9781003594215-5

What distinguishes Gestalt coaching from other approaches is its profound respect for the individual's inherent capacity for self-regulation when provided with enhanced awareness and supportive challenge. By attending to the full spectrum of human experience – cognitive, emotional, somatic and relational – Gestalt coaching enables a more integrated and sustainable development compared to approaches focused solely on behavioural techniques or intellectual understanding. As workplaces continue to evolve in complexity and demand greater adaptability, Gestalt coaching offers a sophisticated methodology that develops not just specific skills but also the fundamental phenomenological awareness and presence from which wise action naturally emerges. Let's explore this approach in more depth.

Key Principles and Aims

The primary aims of Gestalt coaching include:

- Promotion of Awareness: Facilitating heightened awareness and mindfulness of one's thoughts, emotions, bodily sensations and relational dynamics in the present moment
- Integration of the Self: Supporting individuals in integrating fragmented aspects of their personality, emotions and experiences into a cohesive whole
- Enhancement of Personal Responsibility: Encouraging clients to take ownership of their thoughts, feelings and behaviours, fostering self-accountability and empowerment
- Facilitation of Contact and Relating: Exploring how individuals relate to themselves and others, enhancing relational skills and improving interpersonal dynamics
- Promotion of Growth and Development: Assisting clients in identifying and pursuing personal and professional goals aligned with their values and aspirations.

Gestalt Coaching: A Deeper Exploration

Gestalt coaching relies on the phenomenological method, which focuses more on describing experience rather than explaining it. Coaches ask "what" and "how" questions more than "why" questions, directing attention to observable phenomena rather than interpretations or analyses. A coach might ask, "What are you experiencing right now?" or "How do you feel as you talk about this procrastination?" rather than "Why do you think you're procrastinating?" This keeps the focus on immediate experience, where change can occur.

As in most coaching approaches, the Gestalt coaching relationship itself is a powerful vehicle for learning and change. The coach models authentic presence and clear boundaries while serving as a mirror for patterns that might be invisible to the client. The relationship becomes a "safe emergency" – secure enough for exploration but challenging enough to prompt growth. The coach notices how the client relates within the coaching relationship and uses these observations as data about how the client might relate in other contexts. For example, if a client habitually deflects compliments or positive feedback from the coach, this pattern likely appears in other relationships as well. Bringing awareness to this in-the-moment behaviour creates an opportunity for experimentation with new responses.

Present-Moment Awareness

Gestalt coaching emphasises heightened awareness of what is happening in the present moment. This includes awareness of thoughts, emotions, body sensations and the environment. A Gestalt coach helps clients notice when they disconnect from the present – perhaps by dwelling on the past, worrying about the future or intellectualising rather than experiencing. Through various experiments and exercises, clients develop the capacity to stay present with their immediate experience, even when it's uncomfortable.

For instance, if a client is describing a workplace conflict while simultaneously clenching their fists, a Gestalt coach might ask, "Are you aware that you're tightening your hands right now? What happens if you pay attention to that sensation while continuing to talk about your colleague?" This present-moment focus allows clients to recognise patterns as they unfold, rather than analysing them after the fact. It creates opportunities for immediate choice and change.

The Paradoxical Theory of Change

One of Gestalt's most profound insights is that authentic change occurs not when we try to become something different, but when we fully become who we already are. As Gestalt therapist Arnold Beisser expressed it: "Change occurs when one becomes more of what one is, not when they try to become what they are not." In practice, this means that Gestalt coaches don't push clients towards predetermined outcomes. Instead, they help clients fully experience and accept their current reality. Paradoxically, this acceptance creates the conditions for organic and profound change to emerge. For example, a client who constantly pushes themselves to work harder might actually need to fully experience and accept their fatigue rather than fighting against it. Only by acknowledging this reality can they discover a more sustainable approach to their work.

Contact and Boundaries

Gestalt coaching also pays particular attention to how people make contact with themselves, others and their environment. Healthy contact involves clear awareness of where "I" ends and "other" begins – what Gestalt calls boundaries. A coach may help a client examine how they maintain or disrupt contact through various boundary disturbances, such as:

- Projection: Attributing one's own unacknowledged qualities to others
- Introjection: Uncritically accepting others' values or standards as one's own
- Confluence: Blurring boundaries between self and others
- Retroflection: Turning back towards oneself, actions intended for the environment
- Deflection: Diverting energy away from direct contact

For instance, a manager who constantly criticises team members for being "too emotional" might be projecting their own discomfort with emotions. A Gestalt coach would help them recognise this pattern and explore the emotions they've disowned in themselves.

The Figure-Ground Relationship

In Gestalt, human experience is organised into "figure" (what stands out in our awareness) and "ground" (the background context). What emerges as figural indicates what's most important or urgent for the individual at that moment. Gestalt coaches pay attention to what becomes figure for their clients – what they emphasise, what emotions arise prominently or what topics they return to repeatedly. These patterns reveal unfinished business or unmet needs that require attention. They also notice what remains in the background – what clients seem to avoid, minimise or rush past. These aspects of experience often contain important information about blocked energy or disowned parts of the self. For example, if a client consistently focuses on others' needs while leaving their own in the background, a Gestalt coach might highlight this pattern and invite exploration of what makes the client's own self-care difficult to bring into awareness.

Polarities and Integration

Gestalt recognises that human experience often contains opposing polarities – parts of ourselves that seem to contradict each other. Rather than choosing one side over the other, Gestalt aims for integration of these polarities into a more complete whole. A coach can help a client identify polarities in their experience (strength/vulnerability, autonomy/connection or structure/spontaneity) and explore both sides fully. By experiencing both poles, clients discover a more flexible middle ground that incorporates aspects of each. For instance, a leader struggling with being either too authoritarian or too inclusive and consultative might work with a coach to explore both styles fully, ultimately developing a more integrated approach that can draw on both authority and collaboration as needed.

Experiments

Perhaps more than in any other approach, Gestalt coaches design in-the-moment experiments that bring awareness to aspects of experience that might otherwise remain unconscious. These might include:

- Empty chair work: Dialoguing with an imagined person (or part of oneself) sitting in an empty chair
- Awareness exercises: Structured practices to notice sensations, emotions or thoughts
- Exaggeration: Amplifying a subtle gesture or expression to reveal its full meaning
- Role reversal: Taking the perspective of another person in a situation
- Creative expression: Using movement, art or metaphor to express experience non-verbally

These experiments aren't techniques applied mechanically but creative explorations designed specifically for each client's unique situation. They aim to heighten awareness and open new possibilities rather than force particular outcomes.

Applying Gestalt Coaching in the Workplace

In workplace settings, Gestalt coaching offers particular value for addressing the multifaceted challenges of leadership development, team dynamics, organisational change and career transitions. Leaders who engage in Gestalt coaching often develop greater presence, authenticity and relational intelligence as they become more aware of how their own patterns impact those around them. Teams benefit from Gestalt approaches that illuminate system dynamics and facilitate more honest dialogue about difficult topics. Organisations navigating change find value in Gestalt coaching's capacity to honour the emotional dimensions of transition while fostering creative adaptation to new realities. Here's how it can be applied in various work contexts:

For individual development, Gestalt coaching can help with:

- Increasing self-awareness and emotional intelligence
- Identifying and changing ineffective patterns of behaviour
- Developing greater presence and authenticity in professional roles
- Making contact with disowned aspects of self that may be limiting effectiveness
- Finding creative solutions by accessing the whole self, not just analytical thinking

For leadership development, Gestalt approaches support:

- Developing an authentic leadership presence
- Balancing authority with collaboration

- Becoming aware of projections onto team members
- Recognising how personal history shapes leadership style
- Creating psychological safety through genuine presence
- Integrating polarities like strategic vision and operational detail

In a team context, Gestalt coaching facilitates:

- Improving contact between team members
- Recognising and working with team polarities and projections
- Bringing background conflicts into the figure to be addressed
- Developing team awareness of patterns that limit collaboration
- Experimenting with new ways of working together

At an organisational level, Gestalt principles inform:

- Understanding resistance to change as a natural boundary phenomenon
- Working with the organisation as a whole system rather than isolated parts
- Bringing awareness to cultural patterns that have become automatic
- Facilitating authentic contact between different parts of the organisation
- Supporting integration of polarities like stability and innovation

Practical Starting Points

To start bringing Gestalt coaching approaches into the workplace, consider these practical starting points:

1. Enhance awareness through present-moment focus: Begin coaching conversations by centring individuals in their immediate experience. Ask, "What are you noticing right now?" about your thoughts, feelings and body sensations while discussing workplace challenges. This shift helps leaders move from abstract analysis to embodied awareness, revealing insights that purely cognitive approaches might overlooks.
2. Work with polarities: Help employees identify opposing forces they're experiencing (such as structure vs. flexibility and confidence vs. humility). Rather than choosing one pole over the other, support them in recognising both sides as valuable and exploring how they might integrate these seemingly contradictory qualities for more balance.
3. Use the "empty chair" technique: Invite coachees/colleagues to externalise different perspectives in challenging work situations. Have them physically change seats to embody different viewpoints – their own, a colleague's or even conflicting parts of themselves. This creates new insights about workplace conflicts and decision-making dilemmas.
4. Apply the figure-ground concept: Help individuals distinguish between what's prominently capturing their attention (figure) versus what's receding into the

background. Ask, "What's most energising for you right now in this situation?" followed by "What might you be overlooking?" This reveals blind spots and expands perspective on workplace challenges.

5. Experiment with new behaviours: Design small experiments to try first before implementing them at work. For example, if someone struggles with assertiveness, have them practise different communication styles in role-play scenarios, noticing how each approach affects their energy and confidence.

6. Track interruptions to contact: Help individuals identify how they interrupt connections with themselves and others through deflection, projection, introjection, retroflection or confluence. For instance, when someone consistently takes on too much work (retroflection), help them recognise this pattern and experiment with delegation and boundary-setting.

7. Create completion through unfinished business: Guide individuals in identifying workplace situations that feel incomplete or unresolved – whether unaddressed conflicts, unexpressed appreciations or postponed decisions. Support them in finding closure through symbolic acts or direct communication that brings resolution and releases energy for new challenges.

Each of these approaches brings the distinctive awareness-focused, experiential nature of Gestalt coaching into workplace contexts, helping individuals develop greater presence, authenticity and effectiveness in their professional lives.

Gestalt coaching in the workplace isn't about applying techniques but about bringing a better quality of awareness and presence to work relationships and challenges. By focusing on the present experience, clear contact and the integration of polarities, this coaching approach supports a more holistic and authentic way of working that can transform both individual effectiveness and organisational culture.

Further Reading

Bluckert, P. (2018). *Gestalt coaching: Right here, right now*. Open University Press.

Chidiac, M. A. (2018). *Relational organisational gestalt: An emergent approach to organizational development*. Routledge.

Clarkson, P., & Cavicchia, S. (2021). *Gestalt coaching and consulting: Field theory in practice*. Routledge.

Critchley, B., & Casey, D. (2019). *The whole person for the whole organization: Gestalt coaching in action*. Routledge.

Gillie, M., & Shackleton, M. (2017). *Gestalt in coaching: Distinctive features*. Routledge.

Latner, J., & Fodor, I. (2018). *Gestalt coaching for awareness and presence: The gestalt approach to leadership development*. Gestalt Institute Press.

Nevis, E. C. (2013). *Organizational consulting: A Gestalt approach*. GestaltPress.

Parlette, M., & Beisser, A. (2015). *Gestalt theory and coaching: The paradoxical theory of change*. Gestalt International Press.

Rainey, M. A., & Hanafin, J. (2019). *Gestalt coaching methods: Field theory applications in leadership development*. International Gestalt Journal Press.

Siminovitch, D. E., & Van Eron, A. M. (2016). *A gestalt coaching primer: The path toward awareness IQ*. OD Practitioner Press.

Spoth, J., & Gold, M. (2019). *Gestalt coaching approaches for organizational contexts*. Taylor & Francis.

Stevenson, H. (2019). *Gestalt coaching: Developing human potential in organizations*. Routledge.

Wolfert, R., & Sills, C. (2018). *Gestalt approaches to coaching: Working with contact boundaries*. Sage Publications.

Chapter 4

Cognitive Coaching

Cognitive coaching emerged as an extension of cognitive behavioural therapy (CBT), which was pioneered by psychologists like Albert Ellis (1913–2007) and Aaron Beck (1921–2021) in the mid-20th century. CBT focused on the idea that our thoughts (cognitions) influence our emotions and behaviours. It aimed to challenge and change negative thinking patterns to alleviate emotional distress and improve psychological well-being.

Over time, cognitive coaching techniques have become popular not only in therapeutic settings but also in organisational coaching, sports psychology and educational coaching. The principles of CBT have been adapted to help individuals achieve their goals, enhance performance and foster personal development.

Unlike other methodologies that may focus primarily on behaviours or emotions, cognitive coaching targets the thinking that underlies human action and is an approach to professional development that uses this focus on improving thinking processes to enhance decision-making, problem-solving and self-directed learning.

Cognitive coaching is built on the premise that all behaviour is based on perceptions and that by changing perceptions and thought processes, we can enhance mood, motivation and performance. The fundamental philosophy centres on the idea that the cognitive coach serves as a mediator of thinking, not as an expert providing solutions. This approach is deeply rooted in constructivist learning theory, which holds that people construct their understanding of reality rather than simply receiving "wisdom" from others. Let's explore this approach in more depth.

Key Principles and Aims

Like most forms of coaching, Cognitive coaching operates from the belief that people already possess the internal resources they need to solve their problems and improve their performance. The coach's role is not to supply answers but to help individuals access their own wisdom, creativity and problem-solving abilities. This principle manifests in coaching conversations where the coach refrains from offering solutions, even when they might have relevant expertise. Instead, they ask questions that help the person being coached tap into their own knowledge and generate their own insights.

DOI: 10.4324/9781003594215-6

The primary aims of cognitive coaching include:

- Identifying Cognitive Distortions: Helping individuals recognise and challenge cognitive distortions or biases that contribute to negative emotions and behaviours (e.g. all-or-nothing thinking, catastrophising, mind reading or fortune-telling).
- Promoting Cognitive Restructuring: Facilitating the process of cognitive restructuring, which involves replacing irrational or maladaptive thoughts with more rational and constructive alternatives – that is, thoughts and beliefs that are more consistent with logic, reason and empirical evidence.
- Enhancing Self-Awareness: Increasing awareness of one's thought processes, emotional responses and behavioural patterns – and the relationship between each of these – to promote self-reflection and insight.
- Improving Decision-Making: Developing skills to make more informed and effective decisions by evaluating and recalibrating cognitive biases and their related underlying assumptions.
- Behavioural Change: Encouraging behavioural change through the modification of underlying thought patterns and beliefs that contribute to specific actions or habits.

Cognitive Coaching: A Deeper Exploration

Unlike coaching approaches that focus primarily on outcomes, cognitive coaching pays particular attention to the thinking processes that lead to those outcomes. The coach helps individuals become more aware of their thought patterns, assumptions, beliefs and mental models. This focus on cognitive processes is based on research showing that expert performers in any field have more sophisticated cognitive structures – they perceive patterns, organise information and process feedback differently than novices. By developing these cognitive structures, individuals can improve their performance across diverse situations. For instance, when working with a professional facing a complex decision, a cognitive coach might explore questions like "What criteria are you using to evaluate your options?" or "How are you organising the information you've gathered?" These questions help the individual become more aware of and intentional about their thinking patterns and processes.

Cognitive Coaching Aims to Increase Two Particular Internal States That Influence Effectiveness: Thinking Efficacy and Thinking Flexibility

- *Efficacy* – refers to the belief in one's capacity to make a difference and to produce intended outcomes. People with high efficacy set challenging goals, persist in the face of obstacles and learn from setbacks rather than being defeated by them. A coach might help develop efficacy by asking questions that highlight past successes such as "When have you faced a similar challenge and overcome it?" They can also encourage reflection on internal resources by asking "What strengths do you bring to this situation?"

- *Flexibility* – involves the ability to view situations from multiple perspectives and adapt approaches accordingly. People with high flexibility can generate numerous options, consider diverse viewpoints and respond appropriately to changing circumstances. A coach might foster flexibility by asking, "What other ways might you frame this problem?" or "How might someone with a different background view this situation?"

The cognitive coach helps individuals assess and develop both of these states of mind, recognising that different situations may require a different emphasis on a different state.

Facilitative Questioning

Cognitive coaching employs a specific type of questioning designed to facilitate thinking rather than direct it. These questions are open-ended, non-judgemental and focused on cognition rather than emotion or behaviour. Facilitative questions often:

- Begin with "what" or "how" rather than "why"
- Invite reflection rather than quick answers
- Focus on thinking and perceptions rather than justifications
- Encourage the generation of multiple possibilities
- Prompt connections between ideas or experiences

For example, instead of asking "Why did you approach the project that way?" (which might trigger defensiveness), a cognitive coach might ask, "What factors influenced your approach to the project?" This subtle shift invites reflection rather than justification.

Data-Based Interactions

Cognitive coaching also emphasises the use of specific, observable data rather than generalisations. The coach helps the individual gather and analyse relevant data about their performance, which serves as a foundation for reflection. For example, rather than discussing a presentation in general terms ("It went well" or "it was a disaster"), a cognitive coach might ask for specific observations ("What did you notice about the audience's engagement during the different parts of your presentation?") or might share non-judgemental observations ("I noticed that you refrained from asking for questions during your presentation"). This focus on concrete data grounds the coaching process in reality rather than perceptions or assumptions, creating a more objective basis for learning.

Applying Cognitive Coaching in the Workplace

Cognitive coaching offers powerful applications in workplace settings, providing a structured approach to developing thinking skills that enhance both individual performance and organisational effectiveness. Here are some examples of how this approach can be implemented in various work contexts:

Finding Clarity and Direction

Many professionals struggle with information overload and competing priorities. Cognitive coaching can help employees develop mental clarity by improving their ability to organise information, establish priorities and maintain focus. For example, a project manager facing multiple deadlines might work with a coach to develop more sophisticated thinking about how to categorise and sequence tasks. Rather than telling the manager what to prioritise, the coach would ask questions like "What criteria are you using to determine which tasks are most important?" or "How might you organise these responsibilities in a way that aligns with your key objectives?" This process helps the employee develop their own mental frameworks for creating order amid complexity – a skill that transfers across various situations rather than solving just the immediate problem.

Enhancing Decision-Making

Decision-making quality depends largely on the thinking processes that precede the decision. Cognitive coaching improves these processes by helping employees become more aware of their reasoning patterns, biases and mental shortcuts. A coach might help someone facing a difficult decision by asking questions that expand their thinking such as "What assumptions are you making about this situation?" "What additional information might be helpful before deciding?" or "How might you test your thinking about this?" This approach develops more sophisticated decision-making capacities rather than simply addressing the specific decision at hand.

Developing Problem-Solving Capabilities

When faced with workplace challenges, many people jump quickly to solutions without fully understanding the problem. Cognitive coaching slows down this process, helping employees think more carefully about problem definition before moving to solution generation. For instance, a team leader struggling with interdepartmental conflict might work with a coach who asks, "How would you describe the core issue here?" followed by "What other ways might you frame this problem?" These questions help the leader see the situation from multiple perspectives, potentially revealing new approaches. The coach then might explore the leader's thinking about potential solutions: "What criteria will you use to evaluate possible approaches?" or "What might be the unintended consequences of each option you're considering?"

Managing Workplace Relationships

Many workplace challenges involve interpersonal dynamics. Cognitive coaching helps employees develop more sophisticated thinking about these relationships by examining their perceptions, attributions and communication patterns. A coach might help someone navigate a difficult relationship by asking, "What assumptions are you making about this person's intentions?" or "How might their perspective differ from yours?" or "What patterns do you notice in your interactions?" By developing more complex thinking about interpersonal dynamics, employees can respond more thoughtfully rather than reactively to challenging interactions.

Strategic Thinking Development

Cognitive coaching helps leaders develop more sophisticated strategic thinking by examining their mental models about the business environment, organisational capabilities and potential futures. A coach might help a leader explore questions like "What assumptions are you making about market trends?" or "How might you view this challenge from different time horizons?" or "What patterns do you see across these seemingly unrelated developments?" These conversations help leaders develop more nuanced and flexible thinking about complex strategic issues rather than relying on fixed frameworks or past experiences.

Creating Thinking-Centred Team Cultures

Leaders can use cognitive coaching principles to develop team cultures where thinking quality is valued as much as action and results. This might involve:

- Modelling thoughtful enquiry rather than quick judgement
- Creating meeting structures that include reflection time
- Asking questions that develop collective thinking
- Recognising and celebrating high-quality thinking processes, not just outcomes
- Creating psychological safety for expressing tentative or evolving ideas

For example, a leader might begin team meetings with a planning frame ("What do we want to accomplish today and how will we know if we've succeeded?") and end with reflection ("What insights have we gained and how might we apply them?").

Collective Problem-Solving

Cognitive coaching approaches can enhance how teams solve problems together by improving their collective thinking processes. A team manager or facilitator using cognitive coaching principles might:

- Help the team clarify the problem before jumping to solutions
- Ensure that diverse thinking styles and perspectives are expressed
- Guide the team in examining their shared assumptions and mental models
- Facilitate reflection on both outcomes and thinking processes

For example, when facing a complex problem, the team manager/facilitator might ask, "Before we discuss solutions, what different ways might we frame this challenge?" followed by "What information do we have and what information might we need?" These questions help the team develop a more sophisticated collective understanding before moving to action.

Decision-Making Processes

Teams often make decisions based on limited perspectives or without explicit criteria. Cognitive coaching can enhance team decision-making by making the underlying thinking more visible and rigorous. A manager or facilitator might guide the team through questions like:

- "What criteria should we use to evaluate our options?"
- "What assumptions are we making that could influence our decision?"
- "How might someone with a different perspective view this choice?"
- "What potential unintended consequences should we consider?"

This process helps teams develop more thoughtful and transparent decision-making rather than relying on the loudest voice or highest authority in the room.

Also, teams can often move from one project or challenge to the next without fully extracting the learning that has taken place. Cognitive coaching approaches can create the structured reflection that enhances such collective learning. For example, after completing a project, a team might delve into questions such as:

- "What results did we achieve compared to what we intended?"
- "What factors influenced our performance, both positively and negatively?"
- "What patterns do we notice across our work together?"
- "How might we apply these insights to future projects?"

These conversations help teams develop more sophisticated mental models that improve future performance rather than simply celebrating successes or assigning blame for failures.

Practical Starting Points

If you're interested in bringing cognitive coaching into your workplace, here are some concrete ways to begin:

1. Practise non-judgemental questioning: Begin conversations with open-ended questions that encourage reflection rather than directing towards specific answers. Use phrases like "What are your thoughts about . . ." or "How might you approach . . ." to activate the other person's thinking processes and show trust in their cognitive capacity to solve problems.
2. Apply cognitive mapping techniques: Guide colleagues in visually mapping their thinking about workplace situations. Have them create mind maps or flow-charts that externalise their mental models about challenges, decisions or team dynamics. This makes implicit assumptions explicit and creates opportunities to examine and refine thinking patterns.
3. Facilitate cognitive shifts: Support others in moving between different cognitive states – from focused analysis to a broader perspective-taking, or from critical evaluation to creative brainstorming. Help them recognise when they're stuck in one mode of thinking and practise deliberate transitions to access different cognitive resources.
4. Institute reflection cycles: Establish regular, structured reflection practices where employees analyse recent workplace experiences using cognitive frameworks. Guide them through examining their thinking before, during and after significant events to identify patterns, biases and opportunities for cognitive refinement. This systematic approach builds the habit of continuous cognitive improvement.
5. Practise cognitive rehearsal: Help individuals mentally simulate challenging workplace scenarios before they occur. Guide them through visualising not just their actions but also their thinking processes during anticipated situations. This strengthens cognitive pathways, reduces anxiety and prepares individuals to access their best thinking under pressure.
6. Develop metacognitive awareness: Encourage individuals to think about their thinking by asking questions like "What assumptions are influencing your approach?" or "How did you arrive at that conclusion?" This builds self-monitoring capabilities that transfer into everyday workplace decision-making.
7. Foster cognitive flexibility through multiple perspectives: When employees face challenging situations, prompt them to deliberately generate alternative interpretations or approaches. Ask, "What's another way to view this situation?" or "How might someone with a different background approach this problem?" This builds cognitive agility and reduces rigid thinking patterns.

These approaches embody the essence of cognitive coaching by honouring intellectual autonomy while providing structured support for developing more sophisticated thinking processes that enhance workplace effectiveness and decision-making capacity.

Cognitive coaching in the workplace isn't about applying techniques mechanically but about valuing thinking quality as much as action and results. By focusing on developing cognitive processes, this approach creates more adaptable, self-directed individuals and organisations capable of navigating complexity with greater sophistication and success.

Further Reading

Anderson, J. R. (2020). *Cognitive coaching for executive performance: A guide to mental models in leadership*. Harvard Business Review Press.

Auerbach, J. E. (2018). *Cognitive coaching: A success-driven approach to executive development*. International Coach Federation Press.

Diaz, K. A. (2019). *Thinking to achieve: Cognitive coaching in leadership development*. Harvard Business Review Press.

Ellison, J., & Hayes, C. (2020). *Cognitive coaching: Developing self-directed leaders and learners* (4th ed.). Rowman & Littlefield.

Ives, Y., & Cox, E. (2016). *Cognitive behavioural coaching in practice: An evidence-based approach*. Routledge.

McKenna, D. D., & Davis, S. L. (2019). *Cognitive coaching for leadership development: An evidence-based approach*. American Psychological Association.

McMahon, G. (2017). Cognitive behavioural approach to coaching. In T. Bachkirova, G. Spence, & D. Drake (Eds.), *The SAGE handbook of coaching* (pp. 258–270). Sage Publications.

Neenan, M., & Palmer, S. (2021). *Cognitive behavioural coaching in practice: An evidence-based approach* (2nd ed.). Routledge.

Palmer, S., & Szymanska, K. (2018). *Cognitive behavioural coaching: An integrative approach*. Routledge.

Passmore, J. (2015). *Excellence in coaching: The industry guide* (3rd ed.). Kogan Page.

Williams, H., & Palmer, S. (2020). *Coaching with cognitive behavioural therapy: Evidence-based approaches for coaches*. Sage Publications.

Part 2

Leadership Coaching and Case Studies

Chapter 5

Existential Coaching – *Behind the Façade*

Michael stands at the pinnacle of corporate success as Chief Strategy Officer of a Fortune 500 technology company. His professional trajectory has been nothing short of meteoric – a corner office with a commanding view of the city skyline, a compensation package that would have seemed unimaginable to his younger self and the respect (perhaps even fear) of colleagues who hang on his every word. By conventional metrics, he has achieved everything he once set out to accomplish.

The polished exterior – bespoke suit, luxury watch and perfectly styled hair – speaks to a man who has mastered the corporate game. His strategic acumen culminated most recently in landing the Jensen account, a ten-million-dollar deal he personally orchestrated that sent champagne corks flying and promises of record bonuses circulating throughout the company. His professional reputation rests on his exceptional ability to analyse market opportunities, navigate complex negotiations and deliver results that please shareholders and executives alike.

Yet beneath this carefully cultivated professional image lies a more complex story. Michael's drive was significantly shaped by his father's experience as a middle manager who felt perpetually overlooked and undervalued. Growing up, Michael witnessed his father's daily defeat as he returned home from work, and he swore he would never experience that same "particular brand of invisibility." This early imprint set Michael on a relentless upward trajectory, one where external recognition and achievement became the primary metrics of success.

In his earlier years, Michael was a more multidimensional person. He painted, read philosophy and harboured ambitions about creating technologies that would "genuinely improve lives, not just capture market share." These passions and ideals have been gradually sidelined during his 30-year climb up the corporate ladder, to the point where they now haunt him "like ghosts." When his partner recently asked what he was passionate about outside of work, Michael found himself unable to answer – a moment that likely catalysed his current existential questioning.

Six months ago, at what should have been a crowning moment of celebration after landing the Jensen deal, Michael experienced an unsettling sense of emptiness and dread rather than fulfilment. This disconnect between external success and

DOI: 10.4324/9781003594215-8

internal meaning has only deepened since then, leading him to question whether he's truly creating anything of lasting value or merely "moving pieces around a board, maintaining the illusion of progress."

As Michael sits in Eliza's reception area, he finds himself at a crossroads – afraid that his identity has been built entirely on achievement rather than meaning, yet equally afraid of discovering "there's nothing substantial beneath" if he steps off the corporate treadmill. He's beginning to recognise that despite his strategic brilliance in business, he has "somehow avoided creating a meaningful strategy for his own life" – an irony that is not lost on him as he contemplates what might constitute "authentic success" beyond the external metrics that have defined his career thus far.

Behind the Façade

The late afternoon sun slants through the blinds of Eliza's office, casting ribbons of amber light across the polished wood of her coffee table. Across from her sat Michael, the sharp creases of his suit at odds with the slight slump in his shoulders. As the Chief Strategy Officer, he had ascended to heights that would be the envy of many, yet the weight of his success seemed to weigh him down rather than lift him up.

"So," Eliza began, her voice gentle but firm, "you mentioned feeling a certain hollowness lately when you think about your work. Can you tell me more about that?"

Michael shifted in his chair, his manicured hands fidgeting with his watch – a luxury timepiece that measured hours he increasingly questioned the value of. "It's absurd, really," he said with a short laugh. "I've achieved everything I set out to achieve. The corner office, the influence, the compensation package that my younger self couldn't have dreamed of. And yet." He trailed off, looking out the window at the city skyline, monuments to ambition and progress silhouetted against the dying day.

"And yet?" Eliza prompted, allowing the silence to breathe between them.

"And yet I find myself in meetings, surrounded by people hanging on my every word, and I'm thinking: 'Is this it? Is this what I've sacrificed the last thirty years for?'" His voice took on an edge. "I'm respected, feared even. But I'm not sure I'm actually creating anything of lasting value anymore."

Eliza nodded, neither agreeing nor disagreeing, but acknowledging the weight of his words. "When did you first notice this feeling?"

Michael's gaze turned inward. "Six months ago. We were celebrating landing the Jensen account, a ten-million-dollar deal that I personally orchestrated. Everyone was euphoric. Champagne, backslapping, talks of record bonuses. And I felt . . . nothing." He swallowed hard. "No, that's not quite right. I felt a kind of dread, like I was watching myself perform in a play I'd seen over and over."

"That's a powerful metaphor," Eliza noted. "The idea of performing in a familiar play. If your career were indeed a play, who wrote the script?"

Michael's brow furrowed. "I've always told myself it was my script. My choices, my drive," he said. The furrow deepened. "But honestly? I'm not so sure anymore. My father was a middle manager who always felt overlooked, undervalued. I grew up watching him come home defeated, day after day. I swore I'd never experience that invisibility."

"So perhaps the script began as a reaction to your father's story," Eliza suggested.

"Perhaps," Michael conceded, a flash of vulnerability crossing his face before the executive mask fell back into place. "But that doesn't explain this . . . emptiness now. I'm not invisible. Quite the opposite."

"What if we explore not just the 'what' of your career, but the 'why'?" Eliza leaned forward slightly. "You've mastered the game by external standards. But I'm curious – what meaning does this hold for you now, beyond proving you're not your father?"

Michael's jaw tightened, and for a moment, Eliza thought he might deflect or retreat into corporate platitudes about shareholder value and market dominance. Instead, he exhaled slowly, his shoulders dropping as if releasing a burden momentarily.

"I used to believe I was building something," he said, his voice softer. "That each strategic move was part of a larger vision. Now I suspect I'm just moving pieces around, maintaining the illusion of progress." His eyes met hers. "I'm afraid I've become incredibly skilled at something that doesn't actually matter."

"That's a profound fear to sit with," Eliza acknowledged. "Let's stay with that discomfort for a moment. If your work as it stands now doesn't matter in the way you once thought it did, what would matter to you?"

Michael's laugh was tinged with unexpected anguish. "That's the terrifying question, isn't it? Because I'm not sure I know anymore. I've spent so long climbing that I've forgotten what I wanted to see from the summit." He ran a hand through his hair, disrupting its careful arrangement. "My partner asked me last week what I was passionate about outside of work, and I literally couldn't answer. Twenty years ago, I painted. I read philosophy. I had ideas about creating technologies that would genuinely improve lives."

"Those earlier passions – do they still call to you at all?" Eliza asked.

"Like ghosts," Michael replied, the metaphor seemingly surprising even himself. "I keep thinking I should feel grateful. Do you know how many people would kill to have what I have?"

"Gratitude and meaning aren't the same thing," Eliza observed. "One can be genuinely grateful for certain aspects of one's life while still questioning its fundamental meaning."

A heavy silence filled the room as Michael seemed to absorb the distinction. When he spoke again, his voice carried a tremor of raw authenticity that his boardroom declarations likely never revealed.

"I'm afraid," he admitted. "Afraid that I've built my identity on achievement rather than meaning. Afraid that if I step off this treadmill, even slightly, I'll discover there's nothing substantial beneath. And I'm equally afraid that if I continue

as I am, I'll reach the end of my life having been successful but not significant."
His knuckles whitened as he gripped the armrests of his chair. "Either way, there's
a kind of death to face."

"Yes," Eliza said simply. "There is." Rather than offer immediate reassurance,
she allowed the stark truth of his dilemma to exist between them. The recognition
seemed to both unsettle and slightly release something in Michael.

"So, what's the answer?" he finally asked, a hint of his executive's expectation
for solutions evident in his tone.

"I can't give you an answer," Eliza replied, "because the answer isn't something
to be given but discovered. But I can walk with you as you face the questions."
She leaned forward. "You're describing what existentialists would call a moment
of awakening – when the scripts and roles we've adopted are suddenly revealed as
just that: adopted, but not inevitable."

Michael's expression shifted subtly, the corporate armour giving way to a more
essential humanity. "So where do we go from here?"

"We begin by fully acknowledging where you are," Eliza said. "You've recognised a gap between achievement and meaning in your life. That recognition, pain-
ful as it is, is actually a profound opportunity. Now we can explore what authentic
success might look like for you – success that aligns with your deepest values, not
just external metre readings."

"And if I discover that authentic success looks radically different from my current life?" The question hung in the air, heavy with implication.

"Then you'll face choices about how to bridge that gap," Eliza said. "Not all
at once, perhaps, but step by step. The question isn't whether you should abandon
everything you've built, but rather how you might infuse it with renewed purpose – or perhaps, how you might begin to build something different alongside it."

For the first time in their session, Michael's posture relaxed slightly, as if the
mere acknowledgement of his existential crisis had lightened its burden somewhat.
"I've spent my career planning strategic futures for businesses," he said with ironic
self-awareness. "Yet I've somehow avoided creating a meaningful strategy for my
own life."

"Which means you have considerable skills to bring to this new challenge,"
Eliza pointed out. "What would it be like to direct that strategic thinking toward
your own existence, with meaning as the metric of success?"

As the last golden light faded from the office, Michael considered the question,
his face revealing both the tension of confronting deep uncertainty and the first
flicker of something that might, with nurturing, grow into authentic purpose.

"Terrifying," he admitted finally. "And possibly the most important work I've
ever done."

Analysing the Coaching Session with Michael

This fictional coaching session illustrates several core principles and techniques
of existential coaching in action. Let's analyse what transpired from the existential
coaching perspective.

Confronting Existential Givens

The session captured Michael's confrontation with several existential "givens" or the inescapable aspects of human existence:

- *Freedom and responsibility*: Michael is awakening to the full weight of his freedom and the responsibility that comes with it. His realisation that he may have been following an unconscious script (reacting to his father's story) rather than making fully conscious choices represents a crucial existential insight. Eliza doesn't remove this burden but helps him recognise it as the necessary starting point for more authentic choices.
- *Meaning and meaninglessness*: The central tension in the session revolves around Michael's crisis of meaning. His statement, "I'm afraid I've become incredibly skilled at something that doesn't actually matter," encapsulates the existential dilemma of potential meaninglessness. Eliza acknowledges this void without rushing to fill it with premature solutions or suggestions.
- *Authenticity versus inauthenticity*: Michael's description of feeling like he's "performing in a play" perfectly captures what existentialists would call inauthentic existence – living according to external expectations rather than authentic self-determination. His fear that "there's nothing substantial beneath" if he steps off the achievement treadmill reflects anxiety about confronting his authentic self.
- *Finitude and mortality*: While not explicitly discussing death, Michael's concern about reaching "the end of my life having been successful but not significant" shows emerging awareness of his finite existence and the implications this has for how he chooses to live now.

The Coach's Approach

Eliza demonstrates several key aspects of the existential coaching technique:

- *Phenomenological exploration*: Rather than imposing interpretations or solutions, Eliza focuses on exploring Michael's lived experience. Questions like "When did you first notice this feeling?" and "What if we explore not just the 'what' of your career, but the 'why'?" invite deeper phenomenological reflection.
- *Staying with discomfort*: When Michael expresses fear about discovering his work might not matter, Eliza doesn't rush to comfort him but instead says, "Let's stay with that discomfort for a moment." This willingness to remain present with anxiety rather than avoiding it is quintessentially existential.
- *Paradoxical theory of change*: When Michael asks directly for "the answer," Eliza responds that "the answer isn't something to be given but something to be discovered." This reflects the existential view that change comes not from external solutions but from fully acknowledging and taking responsibility for one's current situation.

- *Awareness of choice*: Throughout the session, Eliza subtly emphasises Michael's capacity for choice even within constraints. When discussing potential changes to his life, she frames it as "choices about how to bridge that gap," highlighting his agency.
- *Focus on meaning creation*: Rather than suggesting meaning will be found, Eliza's approach implies that meaning must be created through conscious choice. Her question about directing "strategic thinking toward your own existence, with meaning as the metric of success" suggests that meaning comes through active engagement, not passive discovery.

The session also illuminates several psychological processes central to existential coaching:

Michael's discomfort represents what existentialists call "ontological anxiety" – the unease that arises from confronting the fundamental questions of existence. His fear about stepping off the treadmill or continuing as he is ("Either way, there's a kind of death to face") represents this anxiety in its raw form. Michael is experiencing an awakening to his own freedom and the vertigo-like feeling that comes from recognising the full extent of that freedom and responsibility. His comfortable framework for understanding his life and success is dissolving, leaving him to face the anxiety of making authentic choices. In existential terms, Michael has been living in "bad faith" – denying his freedom by allowing his choices to be determined by external metrics of success and unconscious reactions to his father's life. Michael's sense that something is missing despite external success represents a "call of conscience" – an inner summons to authentic existence. His mention of earlier passions that now call to him "like ghosts" suggests personal values that have been suppressed but not eliminated.

Key Turning Points in the Session

Several key moments represent significant shifts in Michael's awareness: the recognition that his career may have been a reaction to his father's experience rather than a fully autonomous choice, the acknowledgement that he fears discovering "there's nothing substantial beneath" his achievement-based identity, the distinction between gratitude and meaning allows him to appreciate his accomplishments while still questioning their ultimate significance, the reframing of his crisis as "a moment of awakening" rather than a failure or problem to be solved and finally, the shift from seeking external solutions to recognising this as "possibly the most important work I've ever done."

True to existential coaching, Eliza doesn't provide concrete answers or a specific action plan. Several important aspects remain deliberately unresolved:

- The specific form Michael's renewed sense of purpose might take
- The practical implications for his career and current role

- The exact nature of his authentic values that would guide future choices
- The concrete steps to bridge the gap between his current and desired life

This lack of resolution is not a failure, but a deliberate aspect of existential coaching. It recognises that these answers must emerge from Michael's own reflection and choice, rather than being prescribed by the coach.

Outcomes of the Session

The session sets the stage for several potential areas of exploration in future coaching:

- Uncovering authentic values that have been obscured by external success metrics
- Exploring how Michael might reconnect with earlier passions like art and philosophy
- Examining how leadership could be transformed by a more meaning-centred approach
- Investigating possibilities for infusing his current role with greater purpose
- Developing courage to make choices based on authentic values rather than external expectations

Throughout the session, Eliza maintains what existentialists would call a "fellow traveller" stance – not directing Michael's journey but accompanying him as he confronts the fundamental questions of his existence. This stance acknowledges that while the existential journey can be supported, it cannot be completed by anyone but Michael himself.

The coaching session marks the beginning of Michael's movement towards greater authenticity.

Chapter 6

Systems Psychodynamic Coaching – *Beneath the Surface*

James Harrington epitomises the successful modern executive. As the CEO of Meridian Healthcare Group, he has established himself as a formidable industry leader known for his strategic vision, operational discipline and ability to deliver consistent results in a challenging sector. His carefully cultivated executive presence, characterised by controlled emotions and deliberate speech, reflects this leader's belief that appearance and performance are inextricably linked in the C-suite.

Under James's leadership, Meridian has pursued an aggressive growth strategy centred on strategic acquisitions of private healthcare facilities. This approach has yielded impressive financial outcomes, positioning Meridian as a dominant player across multiple regions and earning James the confidence of the board. His reputation in the industry has been built on being "thorough" and "unsentimental" in these acquisitions – terms he prefers to the "ruthless" label that sometimes follows Meridian's acquisition and integration processes.

James began his career with more intimate connections to healthcare delivery, starting as a hospital director where he "knew every department head by name." This ground-level experience not only provided him with valuable operational insights but also served as a stark contrast to his current role, where his decisions impact "thousands of people he'll never meet." This evolution from hands-on manager to strategic executive represents both a professional achievement and a personal challenge for James.

The Memorial Health Centre acquisition represented a particularly significant strategic opportunity for Meridian – the missing piece that would have given regional dominance and created substantial scale efficiencies. After two years of careful relationship building and due diligence, James had positioned the deal for approval, only to see it collapse at the final stage when his own COO, David, raised unexpected concerns about integration costs to the board.

This high-stakes setback provides a window into the pressures James navigates daily. He operates in an industry where the mandate to grow through consolidation creates genuine tension with healthcare's mission of patient care and community service. The board evaluates him on "EBITDA and market share, not on whether staff feel secure," creating a structural incentive to compartmentalise the human implications of strategic decisions.

DOI: 10.4324/9781003594215-9

James's relationship with his systems-psychodynamic coach, Dr. Elena Vasquez, exists outside Meridian's formal leadership development channels. Their monthly sessions occupy a confidential space where James can explore dimensions of leadership that aren't discussed at "industry roundtables." This coaching relationship represents James's hunch that standard executive coaching might not address the deeper challenges he faces.

As James grapples with the Memorial Centre setback, he stands at a pivotal moment in his leadership journey. His initial interpretation of David's actions as simple ambition or betrayal conflicts with his emerging awareness that organisational dynamics might be more complex than he has acknowledged. The question before him is whether he can evolve his leadership approach to engage with these complexities without compromising the clarity and decisiveness that have defined his success thus far.

Beneath the Surface

The corner office on the 22nd floor offered a commanding view of the city, but today the panorama seemed to mock rather than inspire. James Harrington stood with his back to his desk, gazing out at the skyline with a tension that belied his carefully cultivated executive presence. Behind him, seated in one of the sleek leather chairs, Dr. Elena Vasquez waited in attentive silence.

Elena was not Meridian's leadership consultant or executive coach – at least not officially. As a systems-psychodynamic coach, her work with James operated in a space adjacent to, yet distinct from, the company's formal leadership development programme. Their monthly sessions were not on any corporate calendar.

"The board meeting was a bloodbath," James finally said, not turning from the window. His voice carried a controlled anger, the kind that executives learn to harness rather than express directly. "Two years of relationship building with the Memorial Centre, gone. The acquisition fell apart at the final stage."

"What happened?" Elena asked.

James turned, his movements precise and contained. "Officially? Regulatory concerns, financing complications, the usual suspects." He gave a short, humourless laugh. "Unofficially? My COO undermined the entire process. David went behind my back to the board with 'concerns' about integration costs."

Elena nodded, taking in both the content of his words and the tightly coiled energy in his posture. "And how did you respond when you realised what David had done?"

"I maintained composure. Addressed the concerns point by point. Demonstrated why his analysis was shortsighted." James returned to his desk, settling into his chair. "I did what CEOs do – I led. But the damage was done. The seed of doubt was planted."

"I notice as you describe the situation, you're speaking about your role – what 'CEOs do' – rather than your personal reaction," Elena observed. "I'm curious about what you felt in that moment of realisation."

James's jaw tightened. "What I felt doesn't matter. What matters is that a key strategic initiative failed on my watch."

"Perhaps," Elena said, "but I wonder if what you felt might tell us something important about the dynamics at play – not just between you and David, but within the organisation as a whole."

A flicker of impatience crossed James's face. "If you're asking if I felt betrayed, yes. Angry? Certainly. But that's not particularly insightful, is it?"

"It might be," Elena replied calmly. "Especially if we consider why David might have taken this action, and what it might represent in the system."

James leaned forward slightly. "He wants my job. It's not complicated."

"That may be true on one level," Elena acknowledged. "But individuals often carry roles and functions for the larger system. I'm wondering what function David might be serving in the organisational system by opposing this acquisition."

James's expression shifted from impatience to reluctant curiosity. "What do you mean by 'function'?"

"Organisations, like any human system, develop unconscious patterns to manage anxiety," Elena explained. "Sometimes certain individuals become repositories for particular feelings or perspectives that others in the system find difficult to acknowledge. Marcus may be expressing concerns that exist elsewhere in the system but haven't found another voice."

"So, you're suggesting his sabotage might not be purely personal ambition?"

"I'm suggesting it might be more complex," Elena said. "Tell me about the acquisition itself. What would it have meant for Meridian?"

James straightened, shifting into the familiar territory of strategy. "Memorial is – was – the missing piece in our regional network. Acquiring it would have given us overall market dominance. Scale efficiencies. Negotiating leverage with insurers, etcetera."

"And for the people of Meridian? The culture? The way work is experienced day to day?"

A subtle change came over James's expression. "There would have been . . . significant changes. Memorial's operating model is different from ours. More traditional, less efficient. There would have been rationalisation of overlapping services. Some downsizing, inevitably."

"And how has Meridian handled previous acquisitions? What's the narrative among staff about what happens when Meridian acquires another facility?"

James was silent for a moment, his gaze turning inward. "We have a reputation for being thorough. Unsentimental." He paused. "Some would say ruthless, though I prefer to think of it as necessary clarity in a challenging industry."

Elena nodded. "I'm wondering if there might be organisational anxiety about this pattern – anxiety that perhaps isn't being acknowledged or contained through official channels."

"So, David becomes the container for this anxiety?" James's tone was sceptical, but not dismissive.

"It's possible," Elena said. "Systems often find ways to express what isn't being addressed directly. If concerns about the human cost of acquisitions aren't finding legitimate expression, they may emerge through other means – like a senior leader raising last-minute objections."

James leaned back, considering. "Even if that's true, it doesn't change the fact that he undermined me publicly."

"I'm not suggesting it excuses his actions," Elena clarified. "I'm exploring what his behaviour might tell us about the larger system – and perhaps about aspects of leadership that are difficult to hold."

A subtle tension returned to James's posture. "Meaning?"

"In your role as CEO, you carry primary responsibility for the organisation's performance and growth. That's an enormous pressure, especially in healthcare with its competing demands of business sustainability and patient care. It can be difficult to simultaneously hold both the imperative for strategic growth and the human implications of that growth."

James was silent for a long moment. "When I started in this industry, I was a hospital director. I knew every department head by name. Now I make decisions that affect thousands of people I'll never meet." A trace of something vulnerable flickered across his face before disappearing. "The board evaluates me on profit and market share, not on whether staff feel secure."

"That's a profound shift in how you relate to the organisation," Elena observed. "I'm wondering about the emotional impact of that transition – from direct connection to necessary distance."

James's laugh held a note of genuine surprise. "You know, no one ever asks about that. The emotional impact of leadership decisions isn't exactly a topic at industry events."

"Perhaps it should be," Elena suggested. "What happens to those feelings – the weight of decisions that affect people's livelihoods, the distance that grows between you and those impacted by your decisions?"

"They get compartmentalised," James admitted after a pause. "Filed away under 'necessary costs of doing business.' There isn't room for."

"For what?" Elena prompted gently.

"For doubt. For ambivalence." James's voice carried a new quality – quieter, less certain. "The organisation needs clarity and purpose from its leader, not existential handwringing."

"Is that true?" Elena asked. "Or is it possible that acknowledging complexity and even ambivalence might create space for others to do the same – to engage with the real challenges rather than splitting into those who drive change regardless of human cost and those who resist it regardless of business necessity?"

James studied her for a moment. "You're suggesting that by not acknowledging my own mixed feelings about these acquisitions, I'm somehow creating conditions for the kind of split that happened with David?"

"I'm wondering if there might be a connection," Elena said carefully. "Often, what gets disowned or denied doesn't disappear – it often gets projected onto others or emerges in unexpected ways. If there isn't legitimate space for expressing concerns about the human impact of strategic decisions, those concerns might find other outlets."

James turned to gaze out the window again, silent for nearly a minute. When he spoke, his voice had lost some of its earlier defensive edge. "The irony is that I do have those concerns. I just don't see how indulging them helps anyone. The reality of our industry is consolidate or be consolidated. If we don't grow, someone acquires us, and then someone else makes those difficult decisions."

"So, you carry that burden alone," Elena observed.

"That's the job," James said simply.

"Is it?" Elena asked. "Or is that a particular interpretation of the job – one that might actually limit your effectiveness in certain ways?"

James turned back, with a question in his expression.

"I'm thinking about how organisational systems function best when important perspectives aren't split off or delegated to particular individuals or groups," Elena explained. "When the CEO carries all responsibility for tough decisions while disowning their emotional impact, and others in the system respond by either compliance or sabotage, the organisation loses access to its full intelligence."

James considered this. "You're suggesting I need to . . . what? Publicly agonise over the human costs of strategic decisions?"

"Not at all," Elena smiled slightly. "But perhaps create legitimate channels where these real tensions can be acknowledged and worked with rather than denied or split off. What might it look like if both the business imperative and the human impact were held together in your leadership team's conversations – not as opposing forces, but as dual realities that need integration?"

"That's a complicated conversation to have," James said, though with more thoughtfulness than resistance.

"Yes, it is," Elena agreed. "And perhaps the absence of that complicated conversation is part of what created space for David's approach. When complex realities get oversimplified, the complexity often emerges anyway, but in less constructive forms."

James was silent again, the executive mask momentarily giving way to genuine contemplation. "I've always seen my job as absorbing uncertainty so others can execute with clarity. You're suggesting that approach might actually create more dysfunction than it prevents."

"I'm suggesting it might be worth exploring a different approach," Elena said. "One where the real tensions of healthcare leadership aren't resolved by simplification but engaged with creatively. Where the organisation's anxiety about growth and change isn't either denied or acted out but contained and worked with."

"And practically speaking? What would that look like?"

"It might begin with your leadership team," Elena suggested. "Creating space to discuss not just the strategic rationale for acquisitions, but also the legitimate concerns about integration and culture. Not to derail the strategy, but to strengthen it by incorporating multiple perspectives."

James nodded slowly. "And David?"

"David's behaviour is worth examining directly with him, certainly," Elena said. "But also, as information about the system. What made the board receptive to his concerns at that late stage? What might that tell you about anxieties or perspectives that haven't found expression through formal channels?"

James's phone buzzed on his desk – a reminder of the next meeting, the next crisis. He glanced at it but didn't immediately move to end their session.

"When I started working with you," he said with unexpected openness, "I thought we'd focus on my leadership style, communication techniques, the usual executive coaching territory. Instead, we keep circling back to these . . . undercurrents."

"What happens beneath the surface – the unconscious patterns, the unstated anxieties, the psychological roles people take up – often has more influence on organisations than formal structures or stated intentions," Elena replied. "Engaging with those undercurrents isn't a distraction from leadership; it's a different, and potentially more powerful, way of exercising it."

James checked his watch and stood, signalling the end of their time. "I have an executive committee meeting in 15 minutes. Perhaps it's time to have a different kind of conversation about the next potential acquisition on our list."

Elena stood as well. "What kind of conversation are you thinking about?"

"One that acknowledges both the strategic imperative and the legitimate concerns," James said, a new thoughtfulness in his tone. "Not to derail the process, but to strengthen it." He offered a small, genuine smile. "Your words, not mine."

"The words matter less than the willingness to engage with the complexity," Elena said, gathering her notes. "And to consider what you might be carrying for the system that perhaps needs to be more widely shared."

As James walked her to the door, his customary executive confidence was tempered with something more reflective. "Same time next month?"

"I'll be here," Elena replied. "Though I suspect the system dynamics will have shifted by then."

"They always do," James acknowledged, and for a brief moment, something like relief crossed his face – the relief of a leader beginning to see that he need not carry alone the full weight of organisational contradiction.

Analysing the Coaching Session with James

This fictional coaching session illustrates several core principles and techniques of systems-psychodynamic coaching in action. Let's analyse what transpired.

The Organisation as a Container for Anxiety

One of the fundamental concepts in systems-psychodynamic coaching is that organisations function as containers for anxiety, and this is clearly demonstrated in the session:

The failed Memorial acquisition represents a source of organisational anxiety – about growth, change, integration challenges and potential job losses. Rather than being acknowledged and contained through formal channels, this anxiety has found expression through David's "sabotage." Elena guides James to see beyond the interpersonal conflict with David to recognise the underlying anxieties in the system: "Organisations, like any human system, develop unconscious patterns to manage anxiety. Sometimes certain individuals become repositories for particular feelings or perspectives that others in the system find difficult to acknowledge." James's view that his job is "absorbing uncertainty so others can execute with clarity" reflects his attempt to serve as a container for organisational anxiety, but Elena helps him see how this approach may actually prevent healthy processing of that anxiety.

Social Defences Against Anxiety

The session reveals several social defences operating within Meridian Healthcare.

- *Splitting*: There appears to be a classic splitting defence where the "business imperative" and "human impact" are treated as separate concerns rather than integrated realities. This splitting is embodied in the dynamic between James (carrying the growth imperative) and David (voicing human concerns).
- *Rationalisation*: James's language about being "thorough" and "unsentimental" and preferring "necessary clarity" rather than acknowledging the company's reputation for ruthlessness demonstrates rationalisation as a defence against the anxiety of harming others through business decisions.
- *Compartmentalisation*: James explicitly names compartmentalisation as his coping strategy: "They get compartmentalised. Filed away under 'necessary costs of doing business.'" This is a classic defence against the anxiety of holding contradictory realities.

Elena gently challenges these defences not by confronting them directly but by exploring their function and consequences for the system.

Role and Authority

The systems-psychodynamic understanding of role is central to this coaching conversation.

Elena consistently directs attention to James's role as CEO rather than just his personal reactions, asking about what it means to carry "primary responsibility for the organisation's performance and growth." The session explores the tension between the formal aspects of James's role (delivering growth and profit) and the psychological aspects (carrying the burden of difficult decisions that affect people's lives). The conversation also touches on how authority is exercised and challenged within the system. David's move to go directly to the board represents a challenge to James's authority that reveals something about how authority functions in the organisation. James's comment about "indulging" his concerns about human impact suggests he doesn't feel psychologically authorised to integrate these considerations into his leadership, seeing them instead as a potential weakness.

Projection and Organisational Role Analysis

The coaching demonstrates the systems-psychodynamic concept that individuals often carry projections for the larger system.

Elena suggests that David may be "expressing concerns that exist elsewhere in the system but haven't found another voice," functioning as a repository for anxieties others are unwilling or unable to express. James has taken up the role of the one who must be certain and decisive, carrying this function for the organisation and potentially making it difficult for others to express legitimate doubts. He has identified with the projection of the decisive, unsentimental leader to such an extent that he has difficulty accessing his own doubts and concerns, seeing them as inappropriate to his role rather than as potentially valuable data.

Elena helps James begin to see these dynamics not just as interpersonal issues but also as information about the larger system.

Below-the-Surface Dynamics

Throughout the session, Elena consistently guides attention to unconscious and unacknowledged aspects of organisational life.

She introduces the concept that what happens in organisations is often driven by unconscious patterns rather than just conscious intentions and formal structures. James acknowledges they keep "circling back to these . . . undercurrents," recognising the systems-psychodynamic focus on what operates beneath the surface of organisational life. Elena draws attention to the emotions that aren't openly discussed in the organisation, particularly around the human impact of acquisitions. The coaching also explores how what isn't spoken (the concerns about the human impact of acquisitions) doesn't disappear but finds other expressions in the system.

Primary Task and Anti-Task

While not explicitly named, the concept of primary task and anti-task functions is also present in the session.

There's an underlying tension between different understandings of Meridian's primary task – is it to grow and dominate the market or to provide healthcare while respecting the humans in the system? David's last-minute disruption of the acquisition could be seen as anti-task behaviour, but Elena helps James consider whether it might actually represent an attempt to address legitimate aspects of the organisation's purpose that are being neglected.

The coaching helps James begin to integrate these seemingly conflicting aspects of the organisation's task rather than seeing them as opposing forces.

Boundaries and Boundary Management

Several boundary issues emerge during the session.

- *Role boundaries*: The tension between James's former role as hospital director (where he "knew every department head by name") and his current role as CEO shows how changing boundaries affect psychological experience.
- *System boundaries*: The acquisition represents a planned change in organisational boundaries, bringing new entities into the system and creating anxiety about identity and belonging.
- *Authority boundaries*: Marcus crossing boundaries by going directly to the board reveals something about how boundary management functions (or doesn't) in the organisation.

Elena helps James recognise how these boundary issues might be contributing to the system dynamics at play.

The Coach's Approach

Elena demonstrates several key aspects of systems-psychodynamic coaching in the session. Elena pays attention to what emerges in the coaching relationship itself, noting James's focus on his role rather than his feelings and his initial resistance to exploring emotional dimensions. She consistently connects James's personal experience to the larger organisational system, helping him see his conflicts with Marcus as information about systemic dynamics. Elena provides psychological containment for James's anxiety, creating a space where difficult realities can be acknowledged and explored rather than defended against. Rather than confronting James's defences directly, Elena helps him explore their function and consequences, treating them as necessary adaptations that may have outlived their usefulness. The coaching consistently returns to James's role in the system rather than treating issues as merely personal or interpersonal.

Key Turning Points in the Session

Several pivotal moments represent significant shifts in James's awareness.

- *Moving beyond personality*: When James begins to consider that Marcus's actions might represent something about the system rather than just personal ambition
- *Acknowledging emotional impact*: James's vulnerable admission about the shift from knowing everyone to making decisions affecting thousands he'll never meet

- *Recognising split-off concerns*: The realisation that he does have concerns about human impact but has compartmentalised them as irrelevant to his role
- *Questioning role assumptions*: James's insight that his approach to leadership (absorbing uncertainty) might "actually create more dysfunction than it prevents"
- *Integration possibility*: The consideration that both strategic imperatives and human concerns could be held together rather than split off or oversimplified

Outcomes of the Session

The session leads to several important outcomes consistent with systems-psychodynamic coaching.

James develops greater awareness of how individual behaviours (his own and David's) may reflect and affect larger system dynamics. He begins to see possibilities for integrating split-off aspects of organisational reality rather than maintaining rigid separations. James moves towards a more authentic exercise of his authority that acknowledges complexity rather than denying it. He begins to reconsider how he might better contain organisational anxiety by creating legitimate spaces for addressing tensions rather than trying to eliminate them. The session ends with a concrete intention to have "a different kind of conversation" in the upcoming executive committee meeting, suggesting practical application of the insights gained.

Throughout the session, Elena embodies the systems-psychodynamic approach by consistently linking individual experience to organisational dynamics, focusing on unconscious and unacknowledged aspects of organisational life and treating presenting problems (like the conflict with David) as information about the larger system rather than merely interpersonal issues to be resolved. The coaching demonstrates how systems-psychodynamic work goes beyond traditional executive coaching approaches that might focus primarily on James's leadership style or communication techniques. Instead, it addresses the deeper currents that shape organisational behaviour, helping James develop not just new skills but new awareness of how he and others are taking up their roles within the complex system of Meridian Healthcare.

Chapter 7

Gestalt Coaching – *The Present Edge*

Daniel stands at the zenith of his professional journey as the newly appointed CEO of a promising technology firm. Six months into the role he spent 15 years working towards, he has every external reason to celebrate. The board is pleased with the company's direction under his leadership, the financial indicators are strong, and he has achieved the kind of professional success that looks impressive on paper and in boardrooms across the city.

His polished exterior projects the image of the quintessential executive – tailored suit, carefully cultivated confidence and an articulate command of business strategy. Daniel has mastered the language and posture of leadership, having risen through the ranks with a combination of intelligence, determination and an unwavering drive to succeed. His company is making meaningful strides in its technology sector – a fact that should bring him profound satisfaction.

Yet beneath this carefully constructed façade lies a man perpetually "bracing for impact," as if success itself might collapse beneath him at any moment. The physical manifestations of this constant vigilance are evident in the tension that grips his body – particularly across his shoulders and the back of his neck – and in the subtle furrow between his brows that rarely relaxes.

This tension has deeper roots than his current role. As the son of a brilliant but demanding surgeon, Daniel grew up in an environment where "failure wasn't an option." His father's exacting standards created a household atmosphere where achievement was expected, and weakness could not be displayed. This parental relationship shaped Daniel's approach to life and leadership, instilling in him a relentless drive coupled with an internal voice that continually questions, critiques and demands more – even when external validation is abundant.

Even though his father passed away eight years ago, Daniel continues to carry his expectations alongside those of his board, executive team and stakeholders. He has internalised a leadership style based on never showing uncertainty, always having the answers and equating physical presence with commitment. The pressure to maintain this performance has left him exhausted and, paradoxically, disconnected from the very leadership role he worked so hard to attain.

DOI: 10.4324/9781003594215-10

As Daniel enters his coaching relationship with Rebecca, he stands at a crucial inflection point. Despite achieving the professional milestone he long pursued, he finds himself unable to fully inhabit his success or experience the satisfaction it should bring. Instead, he operates from a place of constant vigilance, making decisions from a defensive posture of "don't show weakness" rather than from his authentic values and vision.

The question facing Daniel now is not how to achieve more success, but how to transform his relationship with the success he already has – how to lead not from inherited patterns of proving himself, but from a place of present awareness, genuine connection and trusted self-authority.

The Present Edge

The conference room on the eighth floor offered a panoramic view of the city, but neither occupant was admiring the vista. Instead, Rebecca, a Gestalt coach with 20 years of experience, sat with relaxed attentiveness, observing Daniel, the newly appointed CEO of a technology firm. Despite his tailored suit and the carefully cultivated confidence in his posture, she noticed the tension in his jaw, the way his fingers tapped an irregular rhythm on the polished table and the slight furrow on his brow.

"I appreciate you making time for this session, Daniel," Rebecca said, her voice calm and present. "Where would you like to begin today?"

Daniel's eyes flickered to the window, then back to Rebecca. "I should be feeling on top of the world, shouldn't I? Six months into the CEO role I've been working toward for fifteen years." He gave a short laugh that carried no humour. "The board is pleased with the direction. The numbers are strong. And yet."

"And yet?" Rebecca echoed, not filling the space but inviting him to continue.

"And yet I feel like I'm constantly bracing for impact." Daniel's shoulders rose slightly as he spoke, a physical manifestation of the tension he described. "Like something's going to give way beneath me at any moment."

Rebecca nodded, taking in both his words and his physical response. "I notice as you say that your shoulders are rising. Are you aware of that tension in your body right now?"

Daniel blinked, momentarily surprised by the shift in focus. Then he closed his eyes briefly and took stock. "Yes. It's like I'm physically holding myself up, holding everything together."

"Stay with that sensation for a moment," Rebecca suggested. "What happens if you simply notice that tension without trying to change it?"

Daniel sat quietly, his attention turning inward. "It's most intense across my shoulders and the back of my neck. It's . . . familiar. Like an old companion." His expression shifted subtly. "Actually, it's been with me much longer than this CEO role."

"I'm curious about that familiarity," Rebecca said. "If that tension could speak, what might it say?"

Daniel's gaze drifted to the middle distance, considering. "It would say . . . 'Don't let them see you falter. Don't let them see you're not sure.'" His voice took on a different quality, one that was more urgent.

"And whose voice does that sound like?" Rebecca asked, noticing the shift.

A flash of surprise crossed Daniel's face. "My father's. He was a surgeon. Brilliant, demanding. Failure wasn't an option in our house." He shook his head slightly. "But that's ancient history. I need to focus on the present challenges."

"Actually, I'd like to try something, if you're willing," Rebecca said. "The past might be more present than you realise. Would you be open to an experiment?"

"An experiment?" Daniel looked sceptical but nodded. "Sure, I'm game."

Rebecca gestured to an empty chair beside them. "I'd like you to imagine your father is sitting right there. What would you want to say to him about the pressure you're feeling now?"

Daniel's expression tightened. "This feels a bit . . . theatrical."

"It might," Rebecca acknowledged. "And you're welcome to stop at any point. But sometimes speaking directly to a figure from our past can reveal patterns we're still carrying in the present. You don't have to do anything that feels inauthentic."

Daniel looked at the empty chair for a long moment, his resistance palpable. Then something shifted in his demeanour. "Fine. Let's try it."

He turned towards the empty chair, his posture stiffening further. "Dad." He paused, searching for words. "I've done everything you ever wanted. CEO before forty-five. Leading a company that's actually providing something important." His voice took on an edge. "But it's never enough. I still hear your voice in my head, questioning every decision, pointing out every potential weakness." As he spoke, his words gained momentum and emotional charge. "Do you know what it's like to never feel you can rest? To feel like one mistake will unravel everything?" His hand formed a fist on the table. "I'm tired of carrying your expectations alongside everyone else's."

Rebecca observed the intensity building in Daniel's body and voice. "Stay with that feeling. What's happening in your body as you express this?"

Daniel took a breath. "My chest is tight. My heart is racing." He pressed his fist harder against the table. "I'm angry. Really angry."

"Can you stay with that anger for a moment? Not pushing it away or acting on it – just acknowledging its presence?"

Daniel closed his eyes, his breath coming faster. After several seconds, his fist slowly unclenched. "It's not just anger. There's something underneath it."

"What do you notice beneath the anger?" Rebecca asked softly.

"Disappointment," Daniel said, the word coming as a revelation. "Deep disappointment that no matter what I achieve, I never feel like it's enough – like I'm enough." His voice caught slightly. "And exhaustion. I'm exhausted from trying to prove myself."

"That's a powerful awareness," Rebecca said. "Can you tell him about the disappointment and exhaustion too?"

Daniel turned back to the empty chair. "I'm disappointed, Dad. Not in you – in the relationship we never had. One where I could have been valued for who I am, not just what I achieve." His voice grew quieter. "And I'm tired. So tired of trying to earn approval that never fully comes, not from you, not from myself."

The room fell silent. Daniel's breathing gradually slowed, and some of the visible tension in his shoulders released.

"What are you experiencing right now?" Rebecca asked after giving him space to process.

"A strange kind of relief," Daniel said, sounding somewhat surprised. "And clarity. I've been running the company like I'm still trying to prove something to my father, who's been dead for eight years." He shook his head. "I've been making decisions from a place of 'don't show weakness' rather than from my actual values or vision."

"And if you weren't operating from that place of proving yourself, how might your leadership be different?" Rebecca asked.

Daniel considered this, his expression opening. "I might actually listen more in executive meetings instead of feeling I need to have all the answers. I might be more transparent about the challenges we're facing with the new platform launch." A small smile touched his lips. "I might even take a weekend off occasionally."

"I notice your body language has changed," Rebecca observed. "Your shoulders have dropped, and your breathing is deeper."

Daniel nodded, becoming aware of the shift. "I feel more . . . present. Less like I'm bracing for something."

"That presence is significant," Rebecca said. "I'm wondering if you could bring that same quality of presence to your next challenging meeting. What might that be like?"

"The board presentation on Thursday," Daniel said immediately. "I've been anxious about it all week."

"Let's work with that real situation," Rebecca suggested. "If you were to enter that meeting with this same sense of presence, what might you notice? How might you sit? How might you breathe?"

Daniel straightened slightly in his chair, but without the earlier tension. He took a deliberate breath. "I'd notice the room, the people. I'd be aware of my own reactions without being consumed by them." He demonstrated a more centred posture. "I'd speak from conviction rather than defensiveness."

"And what would that make possible that isn't possible when you're in that tense, bracing state?"

"Connection," Daniel said after a moment's reflection. "Actual connection with the board members as people, not just as judges of my performance." His eyes widened slightly with realisation. "And perhaps more importantly, connection with my own judgment and values. Trusting my own voice rather than anticipating criticism."

Rebecca nodded. "That's the difference between responding to what's actually happening in the present versus reacting to echoes from the past."

Daniel was quiet for a moment, integrating the insight. "So where do we go from here? I've spent decades perfecting this pattern of tensing up and pushing through. I'm not sure I know another way to lead."

"I don't think it's about abandoning everything that's made you successful," Rebecca said. "It's about having more choices – being able to access that drive when it serves you but also being able to set it down when a different approach would be more effective. It's about responding to the present rather than reacting to the past."

She leaned forward slightly. "Perhaps we could end today's session by identifying one small experiment you might try in the coming week – one situation where you could practise bringing this quality of presence into your leadership."

Daniel thought for a moment, the furrow between his brows returning briefly, then relaxing. "The executive team has been pushing for more flexibility in our work-from-home policy. I've been resistant because . . ." he paused, making a connection, "because I equate physical presence with commitment. Another inheritance from my father." He continued, more decisively, "I could open that conversation again, but this time truly listen to their perspective without the automatic resistance. Stay present with whatever discomfort arises rather than shutting it down."

Rebecca nodded. "That sounds like a meaningful experiment. And as you try it, I encourage you to notice not just what happens externally, but what happens in your body, your emotions, your thoughts. That awareness itself can create new possibilities."

As their session drew to a close, Daniel stood by the window, looking out at the city with a different quality of attention. The skyline hadn't changed, but his experience of standing before it had – less above it all, more part of it. The tension in his shoulders hadn't vanished entirely, but he was aware of it now, a signal rather than simply a state of being. "Same time next week?" he asked, turning back to Rebecca.

"I'll be here," she replied. "And I'm curious to hear what you discover when you bring more of this present awareness into your leadership."

Daniel nodded, a genuine smile briefly transforming his features. "So am I, actually. So am I."

Analysing the Coaching Session with Daniel

This fictional coaching session illustrates several core principles and techniques of Gestalt coaching in action. Let's analyse what transpired.

Present-Moment Awareness and Phenomenology

The most fundamental Gestalt principle evident throughout the session is the emphasis on present-moment awareness – which Gestalt practitioners refer to as the "here and now." Rebecca consistently directs Daniel's attention to his immediate experience rather than abstract analysis.

- *Bodily awareness*: When Daniel mentions "bracing for impact," Rebecca immediately draws attention to his physical manifestation of tension: "I notice as you say that your shoulders are rising. Are you aware of that tension in your body right now?" This shifts him from talking about his experience to actually experiencing it directly.
- *Staying with sensations*: Rather than intellectualising or problem-solving, Rebecca invites Daniel to "stay with that sensation for a moment" and simply notice it. This phenomenological approach – focusing on describing rather than explaining experience – allows him to discover the familiarity of the tension, leading to deeper insights.
- *Tracking shifts in awareness*: Rebecca continuously observes and comments on changes in Daniel's physical state: "I notice your body language has changed. Your shoulders have dropped, and your breathing is deeper." These observations help bring implicit experience into explicit awareness.

Contact and Boundary Work

Gestalt coaching pays particular attention to how people make contact with themselves, others and their environment. Several aspects of contact work are evident throughout the session.

- *Self-contact*: The session begins with Daniel having limited contact with his own bodily experience. Through Rebecca's guidance, he develops greater awareness of physical sensations, emotional states and needs that had been outside his awareness.
- *Contact with disowned aspects*: Daniel reconnects with parts of himself he had been cutting off from awareness – his anger, disappointment and exhaustion. As he acknowledges these experiences, his energy and presence shift.
- *Boundary contact*: The session reveals how Daniel has maintained rigid boundaries between his professional and emotional self, between his achievement-oriented identity and his need for rest and acceptance. Coaching creates more flexible boundaries where these aspects can interact.

Figure-Ground Relationship

The Gestalt concept of figure-ground is also apparent throughout the session.

Initially, Daniel's focus (figure) is on external measures of success, while his bodily experience and emotional needs remain in the background. Through the coaching, what's figural shifts to include his internal experience. As the session progresses, previous background needs (rest, acceptance, authenticity) emerge as figures. This shift represents what Gestalt calls a "fertile void" – when letting go of fixed perspectives allows new insights to emerge organically. The session moves towards what Gestalt calls "completion" – Daniel's awareness of his pattern becomes clear enough that he can begin to make different choices. The previously incomplete gestalt (pattern) moves through awareness towards completion.

The Paradoxical Theory of Change

Rebecca's approach embodies the Gestalt principle that "change occurs when one becomes more of what one is, not when one tries to become what one is not."

Rather than directly trying to change Daniel's tension pattern, Rebecca first invites him to fully acknowledge and experience it: "What happens if you simply notice that tension without trying to change it?" The goal isn't to eliminate Daniel's driven qualities but to integrate them with other aspects of himself: "It's about having more choices – being able to access that drive when it serves you but also being able to set it down when a different approach would be more effective." The session demonstrates how increased awareness itself creates change, even without deliberate intervention. As Daniel becomes more aware of his pattern, his physiology and emotional state naturally shift.

Experiments and Creative Methods

Gestalt coaching uses experimental techniques to bring awareness to patterns that might otherwise remain abstract.

- *Empty chair technique*: Rebecca introduces a classic Gestalt experiment by inviting Daniel to speak directly to an imagined representation of his father. This technique moves the work from talking about his relationship with his father to experiencing it directly in the present moment.
- *Resistance as information*: When Daniel expresses scepticism about the empty chair work ("This feels a bit . . . theatrical"), Rebecca acknowledges his resistance without pushing through it. In Gestalt, resistance is seen as information rather than an obstacle.
- *From experiment to application*: The session moves from the empty chair experiment to a real-world application when Rebecca asks Daniel to imagine bringing his new awareness into the board meeting. This bridges insight with action.

Polarities and Integration

Gestalt recognises that human experience often contains opposing polarities, and growth comes through integrating these apparent opposites.

The session reveals the polarity between Daniel's drive for achievement and his need for acceptance regardless of performance. Rather than choosing one over the other, the work moves towards integrating both. Daniel has operated from a position of needing to maintain control and avoid showing vulnerability. The session opens space for acknowledging vulnerability without losing his capacity for decisive leadership. The coaching helps Daniel distinguish between reactions based on past experiences with his father and responses based on present reality. Integration comes not from denying the past's influence but from becoming aware of it.

The Coaching Relationship as a Vehicle for Learning

In Gestalt, the coaching relationship itself serves as a microcosm for the client's patterns in other relationships.

- Co-creation: Rebecca doesn't position herself as an expert with answers but as a co-creator of awareness. She offers observations and experiments, but consistently returns responsibility to Daniel.
- Modelling presence: Throughout the session, Rebecca demonstrates the quality of presence she's inviting Daniel to develop. Her own centred attention provides a lived example of what she's describing.
- Working with what emerges: Rather than following a predetermined agenda, Rebecca works with what emerges in the moment. This includes Daniel's physical tension, his association with his father, his resistance to the empty chair work and ultimately his insight about the executive team meeting.

The Coach's Approach

In the session, the coach demonstrates how Gestalt coaching works not by adding new knowledge or prescribing behaviours but by increasing the coachee's awareness of their existing patterns of being. As Daniel becomes more aware of how he interrupts full contact with himself, others and his environment, he naturally moves towards more authentic and effective ways of being and leading.

Key Turning Points in the Session

Several pivotal moments represent significant shifts in Daniel's awareness. When Daniel first becomes aware of the tension pattern in his body and recognises its familiarity. The moment when Daniel connects the critical internal voice to his father's influence. And when anger gives way to the deeper emotions of disappointment and exhaustion. Also, Daniel's realisation that he's been "running the company like I'm still trying to prove something to my father." And finally, the identification of a specific situation (the work-from-home policy discussion) where he can experiment with a different approach.

Outcomes of the Session

True to Gestalt practice, the session doesn't end with abstract advice or a comprehensive plan but with a specific experiment. Daniel identifies a concrete situation where he can practise bringing his new awareness into action. Rebecca encourages ongoing self-observation: "[N]otice not just what happens externally, but what happens in your body, your emotions, your thoughts." While the session reaches a natural completion point, it also sets up an open cycle that will continue into their next meeting and into Daniel's leadership practice.

In essence, the session isn't about teaching Daniel new leadership techniques but about helping him to become more fully present with himself and others. This presence itself – the capacity to respond to what is actually happening rather than reacting from old patterns – becomes the foundation for more effective, authentic leadership.

Chapter 8

Cognitive Coaching – *Clarity Through Complexity*

Sophia Clarke has built her reputation as the consummate corporate strategist. As the Senior Vice President of Global Operations at Nexus Technologies, she is one of the company's most respected executives, known for her operational excellence and strategic acumen. Her 17-year career trajectory reflects a series of calculated moves and achievements that have positioned her as a rising star in the technology sector.

With a background that includes elite education and progressive leadership roles, Sophia has mastered the art of corporate advancement. Her analytical mind excels at solving complex operational challenges, particularly during times of organisational change. The recent merger showcased her capabilities as she worked overtime to ensure smooth integration of global operations – further cementing her reputation as someone who delivers results under pressure.

Sophia's professional persona is carefully crafted – measured in speech, decisive in action and strategic in approach. Her methodology for business decisions follows a clear pattern: analyse, decide, execute. This structured approach has served her well, earning her consistent praise in performance reviews and the personal endorsement of the CEO. Her track record of success has made her the natural candidate for the COO position in Singapore – a role that represents both a significant promotion and the logical next step in her meticulously planned career path.

Behind this professional façade lies a more complex reality. Sophia is also a wife and mother, with a husband who holds a position at a university and a daughter in her first year of senior school. These personal dimensions of her life have generally remained compartmentalised from her professional decision-making, treated as secondary considerations or practical constraints to be managed rather than core criteria for major life choices.

Now standing at a significant crossroads, Sophia faces a decision that refuses to fit neatly into her established decision-making framework. The Singapore opportunity represents everything she has worked towards professionally – increased compensation, expanded equity, a direct line to the CEO and greater organisational impact. Yet it also demands uprooting her family from their established lives, disrupting her husband's career and changing schools for her daughter at a critical educational juncture.

DOI: 10.4324/9781003594215-11

For perhaps the first time in her career, Sophia finds herself hesitating. This uncharacteristic indecision has prompted her to seek coaching, though not without resistance – her three reschedules of the session suggest an underlying discomfort with the uncertainty she's experiencing. For someone who prides herself on clarity and decisive action, this clouded thinking feels particularly unsettling.

As she enters her coaching session with Marcus, Sophia brings her character-istic professionalism alongside an unaccustomed vulnerability. She stands at the intersection of professional ambition and personal considerations, unsure how to integrate these seemingly competing domains into a coherent decision process. The question before her is not simply whether to accept the Singapore position, but how to develop a more integrated approach to life decisions that honours both her career aspirations and her personal values – a challenge that demands new thinking frameworks beyond those that have carried her to her current success.

Clarity Through Complexity

The executive conference room was empty except for two people sitting at one end of the long mahogany table. Large windows offered a view of the landscaped gardens, now turning golden in the late afternoon sun. Sophia Clarke, Senior Vice President of Global Operations at Nexus Technologies, had removed her suit jacket and rolled up her sleeves – a small but significant gesture for someone known for her impeccable professional presentation.

Across from her sat Marcus, a cognitive coach who had been working with several of the company's leadership team. His notepad sat open before him, but for now, he simply observed Sophia with attentive curiosity.

"I've been putting this session off," Sophia admitted, a hint of frustration edg-ing her normally measured tone. "Three reschedules – I'm sure your assistant is wondering if I'm worth the trouble."

Marcus smiled slightly. "I'm more interested in what you make of the reschedules."

Sophia's fingers drummed briefly on the table. "That I'm busy. That the merger has everyone working overtime." She paused, then added with unexpected can-dour, "That I'm avoiding something, perhaps."

"What might you be avoiding?" Marcus asked, his tone neutral.

Sophia gazed towards the gardens for a moment. "The board wants an answer by next month about whether I'll take the COO position in Singapore." Her voice remained level, but her fingers had stopped their drumming and now pressed firmly against the polished wood. "It's the logical next step. The culmination of seven-teen years of strategic career moves."

"And yet?" Marcus prompted, noticing the tension in her posture.

"And yet I find myself . . . hesitating." The admission seemed to surprise her. "Which isn't like me. I don't hesitate. I analyse, decide, execute." She turned back to meet his gaze directly. "My thinking feels clouded on this, and I can't afford cloudy thinking right now."

Marcus nodded. "I appreciate your directness, Sophia. Would it be helpful to explore your thinking process around this decision?"

"That's why I'm here, even if it took me three reschedules to get here." She laughed.

"Let's start with what you know for certain about this situation," Marcus suggested. "What facts or data points feel clear to you?"

Sophia straightened slightly, moving into more familiar territory. "The role is a significant promotion, and the Singapore operation needs a strong hand after the merger – they're struggling with integration." She spoke with increasing fluidity. "My performance reviews have consistently highlighted my operational excellence and strategic thinking, and the CEO has personally endorsed me for the position."

"So, there are compelling professional reasons to accept," Marcus reflected. "What other aspects of the decision have you been considering?"

Sophia's expression tightened almost imperceptibly. "The personal implications are . . . significant. Moving my family across the world. My husband would need to leave his position at the university. My daughter would change schools in her first year."

"When you think about these personal factors, what process do you use to weigh them against the professional factors?" Marcus asked.

Sophia blinked, momentarily thrown by the question. "I'm not sure I have a structured process for that comparison."

"That's quite common," Marcus assured her. "We often have highly developed thinking systems for professional decisions but less explicit frameworks for integrating personal considerations. Would you be willing to try a thinking exercise that might help clarify your process?"

Sophia nodded, her expression a mixture of scepticism and curiosity.

"I'd like you to imagine two distinct thinking spaces," Marcus explained. "In one space, you're thinking purely about professional considerations – career trajectory, impact, organisational needs. In the other, you're thinking about personal and family considerations. How do these two thinking spaces feel different to you?"

Sophia considered this for a moment. "The professional thinking space feels . . . clean. Structured. I have metrics, benchmarks, clear criteria." Her voice became more hesitant. "The personal space feels murkier. More emotional. Harder to quantify."

"And when you need to make a decision that involves both spaces?" Marcus asked.

"I . . ." Sophia stopped, a flash of insight crossing her face. "I think I've been treating the personal considerations as constraints or obstacles to work around, not as valid criteria in their own right." The admission seemed to surprise her. "That doesn't sound very balanced when I say it aloud."

"It's a pattern many executives develop," Marcus observed. "Not a judgment, just an observation. I'm curious – when you think about successful decision-making in your career, what criteria have you typically used to evaluate your choices?"

"Advancement. Impact. Financial growth. Building my expertise and reputation in the industry." Sophia listed these without hesitation.

"Those are outcomes," Marcus noted. "What about the process of decision-making itself? What makes a well-made decision in your view, regardless of outcome?"

Sophia paused for a moment. "Thorough analysis. Consideration of alternatives. Risk assessment." She frowned slightly. "But I'm sensing there's something I'm missing in your question."

"I'm wondering about your metacognition – your awareness of how you think about decisions," Marcus clarified. "For instance, do you have explicit criteria for when to prioritise different types of values in your decision-making?"

"No," Sophia admitted. "I operate more on . . . instinct isn't the right word. Precedent, perhaps. I've always prioritised professional advancement, and it's served me well." A hint of defensiveness crept into her voice.

"It clearly has," Marcus agreed. "You've achieved remarkable success. I'm not suggesting that approach is wrong – just exploring whether it's giving you the clarity you need for this particular decision." He paused. "May I offer an observation?"

Sophia nodded.

"I notice that when you speak about the professional aspects of this decision, you use definitive, confident language. When you touch on the personal aspects, your language becomes more tentative, and your body language shows more tension. What do you make of that difference?"

Sophia's eyes widened slightly. "I hadn't noticed that." She was quiet for a moment. "Perhaps I'm less confident in my thinking process around the personal aspects because I've invested less in developing that thinking framework."

"That's an insightful hypothesis," Marcus said. "What would happen if you applied the same rigorous thinking to the personal dimensions that you apply to professional decisions?"

"I'm not sure what that would even look like," Sophia says.

"Would you be willing to experiment with a planning framework that might help?" When Sophia nodded, Marcus continued. "Let's try mapping out your decision process more explicitly."

He drew a simple T-chart on his notepad and placed it between them. "Many executives I work with find themselves making complex decisions with sophisticated thinking in some domains but less developed thinking in others. Let's make your decision-making process more visible."

For the next 20 minutes, Marcus guided Sophia through a structured exploration of her thinking, asking questions about her criteria, her information-gathering processes, her methods for evaluating alternatives and her approaches to managing cognitive biases and their underlying assumptions. As they worked, Sophia's expression shifted from polite engagement to genuine interest.

"I'm realising something," she said, studying the framework they'd developed. "I've been approaching this as a binary choice – take the promotion or decline it. But there are other possibilities I haven't fully explored."

"Such as?" Marcus prompted.

"Negotiating terms that would allow my family to transition more gradually. Or proposing a different structure for the role." Her eyes took on a new focus. "I've been so caught in the emotional tension between advancing my career and supporting my family that I've fallen into quite extreme black-and-white thinking."

"That's an excellent insight," Marcus says. "What thinking strategy helped you recognise that pattern?"

"Forcing myself to generate multiple alternatives, not just the obvious ones," Sophia replied. "It's something I do automatically in business strategy sessions, but I didn't apply that same rigour here."

Marcus nodded. "You're demonstrating flexibility – a key cognitive skill. You're stepping back from your initial framing and considering multiple perspectives."

"There's something else," Sophia said, her voice quieter now. "I realised I've been making assumptions about what my family would want without actually exploring it thoroughly with them. I've been projecting my own concerns rather than gathering data." She shook her head slightly. "That's not how I'd approach any other complex analysis."

"What stopped you from applying your usual analytical approach to the family aspect of this decision?" Marcus asked.

Sophia considered this carefully. "I think . . . I've compartmentalised. Work decisions get my strategic thinking. Family decisions get . . . something else. Emotion? Intuition?" She frowned. "But that's a false dichotomy, isn't it? Good decisions integrate both analytical and emotional intelligence."

"Powerful insight," Marcus says, simply. "How might your decision process change in light of that insight?"

"I need to bring the same rigor to understanding the personal implications that I bring to the professional ones," Sophia said with growing confidence. "Actually, engage my family in scenario planning instead of making assumptions. Identify our collective values and priorities, not just mine." A small smile curved her lips. "Gather better data."

Marcus watched as Sophia's posture shifted subtly. "I notice your energy has changed as we've made your thinking process more explicit. What are you experiencing right now?"

"Clarity," Sophia said immediately. "Not about the final decision – that will require more exploration – but about how to approach it." She straightened the papers between them. "And permission, in a way. Permission to bring my full strategic thinking to all dimensions of the choice, not just the professionally sanctioned ones."

"That sounds significant," Marcus says. "What specifically will you do differently as you continue to consider this decision?"

Sophia thought for a moment. "First, I'll create a proper decision matrix that includes both professional and personal criteria with appropriate weighting. Second, I'll schedule dedicated time with my husband and daughter to explore scenarios rather than making assumptions about their perspectives. Third, I'll draft alternative proposals for how the role might be structured to address both organisational and family needs." She paused, then added with a hint of surprise in her voice, "And I'll pay attention to my emotional responses as data points, not distractions."

"Those sound-like useful next steps," Marcus says. "Before we wrap up, I'd like to check on your thinking about your thinking. What have you noticed about your cognitive process during our conversation today?"

"That I have blind spots in how I approach complex decisions that span different domains of my life," Sophia replied thoughtfully. "That I've been using different – and unequally developed – thinking frameworks for professional and personal decisions. And that bringing more conscious awareness to my thinking process itself has already created new possibilities I couldn't see before."

Marcus nodded. "That metacognitive awareness is powerful. It doesn't just help with this decision – it strengthens your thinking capacity for future challenges as well."

As their session drew to a close, Sophia gathered her papers with renewed purpose. The indecision that had clouded her expression earlier had been replaced with focused determination.

"Thank you, Marcus," she said, extending her hand. "I came in feeling torn between career advancement and family stability, but I'm leaving with a clearer path to a potentially integrated solution. More importantly, I understand why I was feeling stuck in the first place."

"You did the cognitive work," Marcus replied, shaking her hand. "I just helped make it visible."

As Sophia walked towards the door, her steps had a lighter quality than when she'd entered. She paused at the threshold. "I won't be rescheduling our next session," she said with a small smile. "I suspect I'll have quite a bit to report."

Analysing the Coaching Session with Sophia

This fictional coaching session demonstrates several core principles and techniques of cognitive coaching in action. Let's analyse what transpired.

Focus on Thinking Processes

The most distinctive feature of this cognitive coaching session is its explicit focus on Sophia's thinking processes rather than on solutions or emotions. Marcus consistently directs attention to how Sophia is processing information and making decisions, rather than on what decisions she should actually make. When Marcus asks, "What about the process of decision-making itself?" he shifts the focus from outcomes to thinking processes. His question about "metacognition – your awareness of how you think about decisions" exemplifies cognitive coaching's emphasis on developing the client's awareness of their own thinking.

The T-chart exercise serves to externalise Sophia's thinking processes, making them visible for examination. This is a classic cognitive coaching technique that allows the client to step back and observe their own thought patterns more objectively. Marcus consistently asks process-oriented questions such as "What thinking strategy helped you recognise that pattern?" rather than content-oriented questions. This helps Sophia develop awareness of which thinking strategies are effective for her.

The Three States of Mind

Cognitive coaching focuses on developing thinking skills that enhance both its flexibility and efficacy.

- *Flexibility*: When Sophia realises she has been approaching the decision as binary rather than considering multiple options, she is demonstrating increased cognitive flexibility, which Marcus explicitly acknowledges.
- *Efficacy*: Throughout the session, Sophia moves from feeling "cloudy" in her thinking to experiencing greater confidence in her ability to approach this complex decision. This growing sense of efficacy is evident when she declares with certainty what specific steps she will take next.

The discussion about bringing the same rigour to personal decisions that she brings to professional ones reflects a developing cognitive skill – the drive for precision and excellence in thinking. Sophia's commitment to "create a proper decision matrix" shows her renewed dedication to developing this approach.

Reflective Questioning Technique

Marcus demonstrates skilled use of reflective questioning – questions designed to promote thinking rather than direct it:

Rather than asking leading questions, Marcus uses genuinely open enquiries like "What might you be avoiding?" and "How do these two thinking spaces feel different to you?" These questions invite exploration rather than suggesting answers. His questions frequently target thinking processes: "What process do you use to weigh them?" and "What makes a well-made decision in your view?" These questions help Sophia become more conscious of her implicit thinking approaches. He also demonstrates a non-judgemental stance. When Sophia admits to treating personal considerations as "constraints or obstacles," Marcus responds non-judgementally: "It's a pattern many executives develop . . . Not a judgment, just an observation." This allows Sophia to examine her thinking without defensiveness.

While this appears to be a standalone session rather than part of a planning-action-reflection cycle, elements of the cognitive coaching cycle are still evident. For example, much of the session focuses on how Sophia will approach her decision – essentially a planning conversation. Marcus helps her clarify goals, anticipate challenges and develop strategies. The meta-level discussion about how Sophia thinks differently about professional versus personal decisions represents the reflective aspect of cognitive coaching. The session concludes with specific planned actions that Sophia will take based on her enhanced cognitive awareness.

Cognitive coaching emphasises the use of specific, observable data rather than generalisations. For example, Marcus notes, "[W]hen you speak about the professional aspects of this decision, you use definitive, confident language. When you touch on the personal aspects, your language becomes more tentative." He's providing specific, observable data rather than interpretations. He also pays attention to the different language Sophia uses when discussing various aspects of her decision, using these patterns as data to reflect back to her. Throughout the session, Marcus notes shifts in Sophia's posture, energy and expression, using them as data points to understand her changing cognitive state.

The Coach's Approach

Marcus demonstrates several key aspects of the cognitive coaching technique.

Rather than offering solutions, Marcus consistently signals his belief that Sophia has the internal resources to solve her own problem, simply needing support to access them. While acknowledging emotions, he keeps the primary focus on thinking processes rather than emotional processing. The T-chart and decision framework provide concrete support for making thinking processes more explicit. Throughout the session, Marcus invites Sophia to reflect on her own thinking, developing her capacity for self-monitoring and self-modification.

Key Turning Points in the Session

Several pivotal moments indicate significant shifts in Sophia's thinking:

- *Domain awareness*: Sophia realises that she has sophisticated thinking frameworks for professional decisions but less developed frameworks for personal ones.
- *False dichotomy recognition*: She realises that she has created an artificial separation between analytical thinking (for work) and emotional processing (for family).
- *Binary thinking breakthrough*: Sophia recognises that she has been limiting herself to a binary choice rather than generating multiple alternatives as she would in a business context.
- *Assumption identification*: She realises that she has been making assumptions about her family's perspectives rather than gathering actual data.
- *Integration of thinking domains*: By the end, Sophia realises how she can apply her strategic thinking skills to the decision while also valuing emotional data.

Outcomes of the Session

By the end of the session, several important cognitive coaching outcomes are evident:

1. Enhanced self-directed learning: Sophia has developed a greater capacity to monitor and direct her thinking processes.
2. Cognitive integration: She has recognised ways to integrate different thinking domains (professional/personal, analytical/emotional) rather than keeping them compartmentalised.
3. More sophisticated decision-making approach: The session has helped her develop a more nuanced, multi-faceted approach to her complex decision.
4. Increased cognitive efficacy: Sophia now expresses greater confidence in her ability to navigate the decision-making process, even though she has not yet reached a final decision.
5. Transfer of learning: The cognitive awareness she developed will likely transfer to other complex decisions in the future.

The session demonstrates the essence of cognitive coaching: not providing solutions but developing the client's capacity for more sophisticated thinking. Marcus doesn't tell Sophia what decision to make but helps her develop greater awareness of how she thinks, enabling her to approach the decision with expanded cognitive resources.

What makes this distinctly cognitive coaching is the explicit focus on thinking processes themselves. Rather than focusing primarily on the content of the decision, emotional processing or behavioural strategies, Marcus consistently directs attention to how Sophia is thinking – her frameworks, her blind spots and her metacognitive awareness. This focus ultimately empowers Sophia to approach her decision with greater cognitive flexibility, efficacy and skill.

Part 3

Team Coaching and Case Studies

Chapter 9

Team Coaching

While both one-to-one executive coaching and leadership team coaching aim to enhance leadership effectiveness, they can differ fundamentally in focus, dynamics, methodologies and outcomes. These differences have significant implications for coaches, clients and the client organisations that engage these services.

Focus and Primary Objectives

One-to-one executive coaching focuses on the development needs, challenges and aspirations of a single leader. The primary objectives typically include individual leadership development, enhancing specific competencies, addressing personal blind spots and expanding specific leadership capacity. For example, this approach can focus on improving personal effectiveness through better decision-making, communication and influence. It can provide crucial support during role transitions, helping leaders and other professionals navigate new positions, expanded responsibilities or career crossroads. Performance enhancement can also be addressed by identifying and modifying specific behavioural patterns that may be limiting or even derailing their effectiveness. Many executive coaching relationships may also explore the deeper questions of legacy, purpose and meaning. Throughout this process, the focus remains on the individual's growth within their organisational context, with organisational benefit occurring through the enhanced engagement and effectiveness of that individual leader.

In contrast, senior team coaching focuses on the collective capacity of the leadership team as an interdependent system. It aims to enhance how the team thinks together and integrates diverse perspectives, improving the team's collective intelligence. Team coaching addresses interaction patterns, conflict management and decision-making processes to enhance the overall team dynamics. Creating strategic alignment through shared vision and priorities may also become a core objective. This approach develops the team's understanding of how they function as a system and influence the wider organisation. Such team coaching builds the group's capacity to lead together rather than as a collection of individual leaders, establishing true collaborative leadership. The focus is on team effectiveness

DOI: 10.4324/9781003594215-13

and organisational impact rather than individual development, although individual growth often happens as a result of the team coaching process.

Relationship Dynamics

In individual executive coaching, a dyadic relationship forms between the coach and the coachee that is characterised by high levels of confidentiality. This enables vulnerability and allows for the exploration of sensitive topics. If effective, the one-to-one format facilitates a deep personal connection and trust between coach and client. This intimacy allows for a focused depth, enabling a detailed exploration of personal histories, emotions and motivations that may be influencing their leadership behaviour. Psychological safety is created with clear boundaries, making it a secure space for this depth of personal development. Accountability in this context is direct and personal between the coach and coachee. The relationship serves as both a container for development and a laboratory for exploring new leadership patterns in a safe environment.

Team coaching involves complex multi-directional relationships where the coach interacts with the team as a whole as well as subgroups and individual team members. These relationship dynamics may well include public vulnerability, as team members explore and discuss strengths and limitations in front of their peers. Establishing collective psychological safety becomes more complex, requiring trust among all team members, not just with the coach. The coach must manage parallel relationships with multiple stakeholders simultaneously while navigating both overt and covert power dynamics that influence the coaching interaction. Boundary complexity increases exponentially with multiple formal and informal boundaries to navigate, as the coach must build trust with the entire system while managing the intricate interpersonal dynamics that emerge when multiple leaders interact in a development context.

Process and Methodology

Individual executive coaching typically follows a process that includes personalised assessment through in-depth exploration of the individual's leadership style, strengths, challenges and motivations. Goal setting occurs privately, with confidential development objectives established between coach and client. Interventions are tailored specifically to the individual's learning style and needs, allowing for a highly customised development experience. The coaching relationship provides protected reflection time, creating a designated space for deep individual exploration that busy executives rarely experience elsewhere. Progress tracking occurs incrementally, with regular reviews of personal development against established goals. Throughout this process, the methodology can be deeply adapted to the individual executive's context, learning style and pace.

Team coaching requires more structured processes to accommodate multiple participants. It may begin with a team assessment, evaluating the collective capabilities, dynamics and effectiveness rather than focusing on individual competencies alone. Goal negotiation occurs publicly, with joint establishment of team development priorities that all members contribute to and commit to pursuing. Group interventions are designed for collective participation and learning, engaging the entire team simultaneously. Much of the learning occurs through real-time practice, working with live team dynamics as they emerge within the sessions. The coach helps with systemic pattern identification, recognising repeated interaction patterns across the team that may influence performance, good and bad. Team coaching frequently incorporates work with live business issues, using actual strategic challenges as vehicles for team development. The methodology must accommodate multiple learning styles simultaneously while maintaining momentum for the entire team.

Contracting and Boundaries

Contracting in individual coaching establishes clear confidentiality parameters through detailed agreements about what information remains private versus what might be shared with sponsors or stakeholders. Stakeholder alignment is relatively direct, typically involving just the coachee, their supervisor and possibly HR representatives. The development focus remains specific, with targeted objectives tied to individual growth and performance. Timeline flexibility allows for adjusting the schedule and duration based on progress and emerging needs. Contracts can include defined completion criteria with clear indicators for when coaching objectives have been achieved. Boundaries are also more easily maintained due to the limited number of stakeholders and clearly defined roles in the coaching relationship.

Team coaching contracts must address more complex parameters, including both collective and individual confidentiality – clarifying what happens in full team settings versus any individual conversations that might occur offline. Multiple stakeholders must be managed, balancing the sometimes competing needs of the team leader, individual team members and broader organisational expectations. Objectives operate at dual levels, addressing team effectiveness goals alongside team-wide individual development needs. The contract must clarify coaching authority in relation to existing team dynamics, particularly how coaching input integrates with formal leadership roles. Evaluation becomes more complex as it requires metrics that measure both team process improvements and tangible business outcomes. Boundary management also grows more challenging as the coach navigates pre-existing relationships and hierarchies within the team. All of these contracting elements can require ongoing renegotiation as team dynamics evolve through the coaching process.

Coach Capabilities and Skills

The key for an individual coach is having deep relationship-building capabilities and establishing trust quickly with senior leaders who often have limited time and patience for the development processes. Personal development expertise is crucial, including understanding individual change processes and adult development patterns. Psychological insight also helps in recognising how personal history, personality and mindsets affect leadership behaviour. Facilitating vertical development – that is, supporting growth in complexity of mind and perspective-taking – becomes important for senior executives facing increasingly complex challenges. In addition, individual feedback skill allows for delivering challenging observations in ways that maintain the coaching relationship. Personal presence, the capacity to be fully present with one person's experience, forms the foundation of effective one-to-one coaching. And, while organisational awareness matters, the primary skill is working deeply with one leader at a time.

Team coaches, on the other hand, require a different, though overlapping, set of capabilities. Group dynamics expertise becomes essential, including understanding team development stages and collective behaviour patterns. Systems thinking allows for recognising interconnections, feedback loops and emergent properties of teams as complex adaptive systems. Multi-stakeholder management skills also help in balancing diverse needs across different team members with varying priorities and perspectives. Conflict facilitation also becomes crucial for working productively with tensions that inevitably emerge among team members. In addition, polarity management helps teams navigate tensions that cannot be resolved but must be managed over time. Facilitating this collective intelligence involves drawing out and integrating diverse perspectives into coherent team thinking. Ultimately, the team coach must manage greater complexity while maintaining focus on collective outcomes that serve the organisation.

Outcomes and Impact

Individual executive coaching typically delivers transformed leadership identity, creating fundamental shifts in how the executive sees themselves as a leader. The coaching client may develop:

- An expanded behavioural repertoire with new approaches to challenging situations
- Enhanced self-awareness through greater recognition of strengths, limitations and emotional triggers
- Specific leadership competencies in targeted areas identified as development priorities
- Personal sustainability through better boundaries, energy management and practices that support leadership longevity

Many executives also experience career advancement as coaching prepares them for next-level responsibilities or roles. But ultimately, the organisational impact of individual coaching occurs primarily through the executive's enhanced influence on their team and organisation as they apply new insights and behaviours.

Team coaching aims for broader organisational outcomes, such as:

- Aligned strategic direction through shared clarity about priorities and future vision
- Improved collective decision-making as the team develops more effective ways to integrate diverse perspectives
- Enhanced team dynamics as members develop better approaches to conflict management, trust-building and collaboration
- The senior team delivering more coherent leadership messages with consistent communication throughout the organisation
- A strengthened organisational culture through the modelling of desired behaviours at the senior level

Overall, business performance often improves through better execution resulting from more coordinated leadership efforts. The impact of team coaching occurs directly at the team level but then, crucially, ripples throughout the organisation through the team's collective influence on systems, processes and culture.

Challenges and Complexities

Individual coaching faces several distinct challenges. For instance, transfer of learning can be difficult, requiring specific attention to ensure insights translate to real-world leadership situations beyond the coaching conversation. Organisational constraints may sometimes limit the executive's change capacity despite the development of their personal insights and intentions. Development occurs somewhat in isolation from the team context, potentially creating a disconnection between individual growth and team needs. Resistance to feedback can emerge when examining blind spots, as deep personal defences may arise when exploring sensitive areas. Measuring ROI can also present ongoing challenges, as organisations seek clear connections between coaching investments and business outcomes. So, the primary challenge of individual coaching is connecting personal development to organisational impact in meaningful and sustainable ways.

Team coaching, on the other hand, confronts more complex systemic challenges. Power dynamics require careful management, as hierarchy and authority relationships affect team interaction in both visible and invisible ways. Psychological safety often varies across team members, creating uneven willingness to be vulnerable and authentic in the group setting. Compounding this is the fact that team composition can change through member departures or additions. This can significantly disrupt the coaching process and require recalibration. Even within stable teams, there may be uneven engagement among team members, which can create an imbalance in the development process. Some members are embracing the work, while others remain resistant or on the periphery. Or collective resistance patterns might emerge as the team develops shared defence mechanisms against addressing difficult issues. Then there are competing priorities that can create tension between team development needs and urgent business demands. In the end, the primary challenge of team coaching is to create sustainable change in a complex human system that is embedded within a larger human system with all of its multiple connections and interdependencies.

When Each Approach Is Most Effective

One-to-one executive coaching works best when an individual leader faces specific transition challenges or development needs that require focused attention. It proves particularly valuable when personal barriers or blind spots are limiting leadership effectiveness in ways that targeted individual work can address. Situations that require confidential exploration of sensitive leadership issues can certainly benefit from the privacy of individual coaching. Leaders defining or refining their authentic leadership approach often need the reflective space of one-to-one coaching to explore their values, purpose and leadership identity. When preparation for significant role advancement becomes a priority, individual coaching can provide tailored support for the specific challenges of the new position. In sum, organisations benefit most from individual coaching when individual behaviour change by key leaders would significantly impact and improve organisational outcomes.

Senior leadership team coaching, however, works best when organisations face complex challenges requiring truly integrated leadership rather than siloed decision-making. Teams lacking alignment around strategy or purpose can benefit from the collective focus of team coaching to create shared direction. When fragmentation or silos exist among senior leaders, team coaching can help bridge divides to build a more collaborative capacity. Also, teams that have ineffective collective decision-making processes may discover that they can develop more sophisticated approaches through team coaching. Where leadership impact on culture needs strengthening, or when the senior team needs to model behaviours that they wish to see, organisations can benefit from team coaching that helps the senior leaders demonstrate these desired behaviours or mindsets. Finally, when leadership succession and continuity become organisational priorities, team coaching can build bench strength and enhance leadership capacity.

Complementary Integration

In many organisational contexts, the most effective approach combines both individual and team coaching in complementary ways that leverage the strengths of each methodology. On the one hand, individual coaching may prepare executives to participate more effectively in team coaching by addressing personal limitations that might otherwise hinder collective work. On the other hand, team coaching often identifies individual development needs that are best addressed through subsequent one-to-one work, creating a natural feedback loop between the modalities. Individual coaching can support leaders in implementing insights gained from team sessions, providing personalised guidance for applying team-level agreements to specific leadership challenges. Team coaching can then reinforce and amplify individual development by creating a supportive context where new behaviours can be practised and refined. Thus, combined approaches ensure that both personal growth and collective effectiveness are addressed, recognising that organisational success requires both strong individual leaders and high-performing leadership teams.

The most sophisticated leadership development strategies recognise that individual and team coaching serve different purposes but can create powerful synergies when thoughtfully integrated. By understanding the distinct contributions of each approach, organisations can design comprehensive leadership development programmes that build both individual and collective leadership capacity. This integrated approach acknowledges the reality that leaders operate both as individuals with unique development needs and as members of teams that must function effectively together to deliver organisational results.

Strengths and Weaknesses of Team Coaching Approaches

Now, let's consider our four main coaching approaches as they might be applied to team coaching.

Existential Team Coaching

Existential team coaching brings philosophical depth to leadership teams by focusing on collective purpose, authentic collaboration and shared meaning-making. This approach invites leadership teams to explore fundamental questions about their existence as a team, the meaning of their collective work and how they exercise freedom and responsibility in the face of organisational challenges. Rather than merely addressing functional effectiveness, existential team coaching helps leadership teams confront essential questions about why they exist, what they truly stand for and how they create authentic impact together.

The primary strength of existential team coaching lies in its ability to create profound alignment around shared purpose and values. When leadership teams engage with existential questions together, they develop deeper connections based on mutual understanding of what truly matters beyond immediate business metrics. This shared exploration of purpose creates stronger bonds that can withstand organisational pressures and conflicts. Existential coaching also excels at helping leadership teams navigate ambiguity and uncertainty by developing collective comfort within the inherent limitations of knowledge and control. Teams learn to make authentic choices together without false certainty, an increasingly valuable capacity in volatile business environments. Another significant advantage is the approach's ability to address the anxiety that often emerges during major organisational transitions. By providing frameworks for understanding and working with transition anxiety, existential coaching can help leadership teams maintain cohesion and direction through transformational change.

However, existential team coaching faces several notable challenges. The philosophical nature of the approach may encounter resistance from action-oriented leadership teams seeking immediate, practical solutions to business problems. The language and concepts of existential coaching can sometimes feel abstract or disconnected from everyday business concerns, especially in organisations with strongly pragmatic cultures. The approach requires considerable time commitment for deep exploration, which may conflict with the intense time pressures most leadership teams operate under. Additionally, existential team coaching demands significant vulnerability from team members, asking them to share personal values and concerns in a group setting. This vulnerability requirement can be particularly challenging in competitive leadership environments where showing uncertainty might be perceived as a weakness. The approach also presents measurement difficulties. Organisations seeking clear, quantifiable ROI may struggle to evaluate the impact of existential team coaching through traditional forms of assessment, as profound shifts in team consciousness and the authentic collaboration it fosters do not readily translate to conventional metrics.

The contextual effectiveness of existential team coaching varies considerably. It proves most valuable when leadership teams face questions of fundamental direction and purpose, such as during organisational transformation, mission redefinition or values realignment. It's particularly suited to mature teams with established trust and leaders who value reflective practice. Conversely, it may be less effective with newly formed teams still establishing basic working relationships or in crises requiring immediate tactical responses. Despite these limitations, existential team coaching offers unique value by connecting leadership teams to deeper purpose and meaning, which can provide sustainable energy and direction for long-term organisational impact.

Systems Psychodynamic Team Coaching

Systems psychodynamic team coaching brings together systems thinking and psychodynamic understanding to help leadership teams recognise how unconscious processes influence their collective functioning. This approach explores how the team operates as a system embedded within larger organisational systems, examining both conscious and unconscious patterns that shape team dynamics. Systems psychodynamic coaches help leadership teams understand how they may unconsciously enact organisational dynamics, carry projections from other parts of the system and develop defensive routines that protect against anxiety but limit effectiveness. This approach reveals how leadership teams both reflect and influence the unconscious life of their organisations.

A primary strength of systems psychodynamic team coaching is its unparalleled capacity to make visible the invisible forces shaping team behaviour. Leadership teams gain insight into patterns they were previously unable to see, including how they might unconsciously sabotage their own stated objectives.

This heightened awareness creates new possibilities for breaking recurring cycles that have resisted more surface-level interventions. The approach also excels at boundary management, helping leadership teams understand and navigate the complex boundaries between team and organisation, between different functions and between formal and informal authority. Teams also develop a more sophisticated understanding of their role in the wider system and how to manage their boundaries more effectively. Additionally, systems psychodynamic coaching provides powerful frameworks for understanding resistance to change, revealing how apparent resistance often reflects unaddressed anxieties or unconscious organisational dynamics rather than mere opposition. This understanding can help leadership teams develop more effective change strategies that address underlying concerns rather than just managing surface-level behaviours.

However, systems psychodynamic team coaching faces significant challenges in application. The approach's complex theoretical foundations can create barriers to entry, particularly for leadership teams unaccustomed to psychological language or concepts. The terminology and frameworks may initially seem foreign to business leaders, requiring careful translation into accessible language. The approach can also provoke considerable anxiety as it brings unconscious material into conscious awareness. Leadership teams may resist the discomfort that comes with examining unhelpful patterns they've collectively developed. It should also be noted that systems psychodynamic coaching requires sophisticated facilitation skills to contain the anxiety that emerges when examining unconscious dynamics. Coaches without adequate training may struggle to manage the complex emotions and resistance that often arise. Additionally, the approach requires significant time commitment for deep pattern recognition and processing, potentially conflicting with the immediate results orientation of many organisations. The focus on unconscious dynamics and systemic patterns can sometimes seem removed from practical business concerns if not explicitly connected to organisational outcomes. Without these connections, leadership teams may question the relevance of the work to their performance challenges.

Systems psychodynamic team coaching proves most effective in specific contexts. It offers particular value when leadership teams face recurring problems that have resisted solution, suggesting unconscious dynamics at play. It's especially powerful during organisational transitions, mergers or restructurings where anxiety runs high and systemic patterns become more visible. The approach works best with leadership teams that have some psychological mindedness and willingness to explore beyond surface presentations. It may be less effective with teams strongly resistant to psychological perspectives or organisations with cultures that dismiss the relevance of unconscious processes. Despite these contextual limitations, systems psychodynamic coaching offers unique insights into the deeper currents influencing team effectiveness that other approaches might entirely miss.

Gestalt Team Coaching

Gestalt team coaching brings experiential, present-moment awareness to leadership teams, focusing on immediate experience rather than abstract analysis. This approach helps teams develop a heightened awareness of how they interact, make contact and create meaning together in real time. Gestalt team coaches utilise creative experiments, spatial arrangements and awareness practices to assist leadership teams in recognising patterns in their collective functioning as they emerge in the here and now. Rather than discussing team dynamics theoretically, Gestalt coaches create conditions where teams can directly experience and experiment with new ways of working together during the coaching sessions themselves.

A significant strength of Gestalt team coaching lies in its embodied, experiential nature. Leadership teams don't just talk about changing their dynamics; they actually experience new ways of interacting within the coaching sessions themselves. This experiential learning creates powerful shifts that purely conversational approaches rarely achieve. The approach excels in boundary awareness, helping teams recognise how they create and maintain boundaries between different functions, hierarchical levels and external stakeholders. This boundary clarity enhances the team's ability to manage complex stakeholder relationships more effectively. Gestalt team coaching brings exceptional present-moment awareness to team interactions, revealing patterns that usually operate outside of conscious awareness. Teams develop the capacity to notice in real time how they make decisions, handle conflicts and include or exclude voices. This immediate awareness creates choice points for changing unproductive patterns as they occur rather than analysing them afterward. Additionally, the creative experiments central to Gestalt work can break through entrenched team dynamics that have resisted more conventional interventions. Physical arrangements, role plays and other experiential techniques create insights and possibilities that conversation alone rarely generates.

However, Gestalt team coaching can also face several notable challenges. The experiential approach may initially seem foreign or uncomfortable to leadership teams accustomed to more intellectual or analytical interactions. Some team members may resist what they perceive as "touchy-feely" approaches, particularly in organisations with strong rational cultures. Gestalt work requires a willingness to engage in experiential learning that can initially feel uncomfortable or unfamiliar. The approach also demands sophisticated facilitation skills to design appropriate experiments and manage the intense emotions that often emerge. Poorly designed or facilitated experiences can seem artificial or disconnected from business realities, potentially undermining the approach's credibility. Gestalt team coaching involves considerable vulnerability as team members reveal their immediate experiences and reactions. This vulnerability requirement can be particularly challenging in low-trust teams or competitive environments where showing authentic reactions might feel unsafe. Additionally, the focus on present-moment experience may sometimes come at the expense of strategic perspective or historical context.

Without careful integration, teams might gain powerful insights about current patterns without connecting them to the broader organisational history or its future direction.

Gestalt team coaching demonstrates particular effectiveness in specific contexts. It proves especially valuable when leadership teams have become stuck in repetitive patterns that intellectual understanding alone hasn't resolved. The approach works well with teams experiencing communication breakdowns, polarisation or conflict, where embodied awareness can reveal the underlying contact patterns that are maintaining these dynamics. Gestalt coaching shows considerable strength in helping newly formed leadership teams establish effective contact patterns and working relationships through direct experience rather than abstract agreements. It's particularly useful when leadership teams need to develop greater present-moment awareness and responsiveness to emerging situations. However, the approach may be less effective with teams strongly resistant to experiential methods or in organisations where vulnerability is perceived as weakness rather than strength. Despite these contextual limitations, Gestalt team coaching offers unique value through its capacity to create immediate, embodied awareness and experimentation that can transform team dynamics from the inside out.

Cognitive Team Coaching

Cognitive team coaching focuses on helping leadership teams recognise and refine their collective thinking patterns and decision-making processes by examining how they process information, make judgements, solve problems and reach conclusions together. Cognitive team coaches help leadership teams identify mental models, cognitive biases and thinking patterns that all influence their collective effectiveness. Rather than focusing primarily on interpersonal dynamics or emotional patterns, cognitive team coaching emphasises developing greater awareness and sophistication in how the team thinks together about complex challenges.

A primary strength of cognitive team coaching lies in its accessibility and acceptability in business contexts. The approach's focus on thinking patterns and decision processes aligns well with corporate environments that value analytical rigour and strategic thinking. Leadership teams often readily engage with cognitive frameworks that help them improve their collective intelligence and decision quality. The approach excels at making thinking patterns visible and discussable within the team. By mapping different mental models and decision approaches, cognitive coaching helps leadership teams recognise how diversity in thinking can become either a source of conflict or a strategic advantage, depending on how it's managed. This approach also provides practical frameworks for addressing specific business challenges through improved thinking. Its problem-solving orientation appeals to leadership teams seeking tangible applications and solutions to current issues. Additionally, cognitive team coaching helps teams develop metacognition – thinking about their thinking – which enhances their capacity for self-correction and continuous improvement in their decision processes.

However, cognitive team coaching faces several notable limitations. The cognitive focus may inadvertently reinforce leadership teams' tendency to intellectualise rather than address emotional or relational dimensions of team effectiveness. Teams may gain a sophisticated understanding of their thinking patterns without addressing underlying trust issues or power dynamics that significantly influence their functioning. The approach can sometimes oversimplify complex team dynamics into thinking problems alone, potentially neglecting systemic, emotional or cultural factors that thinking changes alone cannot address. Cognitive team coaching may also give insufficient attention to how thinking patterns are embodied in team members' physical and emotional experiences. This limitation can result in cognitive insights without the embodied integration necessary for sustainable change in team behaviour. Additionally, the approach's emphasis on rational analysis may not adequately address the meaning and purpose questions that often arise in leadership teams facing significant change or transition. Without integration with other dimensions, cognitive coaching might produce more effective thinking without addressing deeper questions of why the team exists and what ultimately matters in their work together.

Cognitive team coaching demonstrates particular effectiveness in some specific contexts. It proves especially valuable when leadership teams face complex strategic decisions that require the integration of diverse perspectives and information sources. The approach works well with teams experiencing decision paralysis, overthinking or recurring cognitive traps that limit their effectiveness. Cognitive coaching shows considerable strength in helping leadership teams develop more sophisticated approaches to scenario planning and strategic forecasting. It's particularly useful when teams need to develop shared language and frameworks for thinking about complex business challenges together. The approach may be less effective, however, when team challenges stem primarily from emotional conflicts, power struggles or purpose misalignment rather than thinking patterns. In these cases, cognitive coaching would need integration with other approaches to address the full spectrum of team dynamics. Despite these contextual limitations, cognitive team coaching offers valuable tools for enhancing leadership teams' collective intelligence and decision-making quality in increasingly complex business environments.

Integration in Leadership Team Coaching Practice

While each of these approaches offers distinct value, particularly effective team coaches will often integrate elements from multiple approaches to address the multidimensional nature of leadership team effectiveness. Such integration recognises that teams function simultaneously at cognitive, emotional, relational, systemic and existential levels. An integrated approach might combine cognitive mapping of team thinking patterns with Gestalt awareness of how these patterns manifest in present-moment team interactions. It might blend systems' psychodynamic understanding of unconscious team dynamics with existential exploration of the team's core purpose and values. The most effective leadership team coaching often draws judiciously from multiple approaches based on the specific needs, context and readiness of the particular team.

The most sophisticated team coaches maintain flexibility in their approach, recognising when a leadership team needs cognitive clarity, present-moment awareness, systems understanding or reconnecting with its values or purpose. Rather than rigidly applying a single methodology, they develop an integrated coaching stance that can address the full spectrum of leadership team development. This integration allows coaches to meet teams where they are most receptive while gradually expanding their capacity to work effectively across multiple dimensions of team functioning.

Ultimately, leadership teams are complex human systems operating in increasingly challenging organisational environments. Their development requires approaches that can address this complexity with sufficient depth and sophistication. Whether through one primary approach or thoughtful integration of multiple perspectives, effective leadership team coaching creates conditions where teams can develop greater awareness, purpose and effectiveness in fulfilling their critical organisational role.

Case Study: Somatech Pharmaceuticals

To illustrate the different approaches applied to teams, we will observe the same leadership team addressing the same issue using all four coaching methodologies. This will highlight the differences and similarities of each approach and illustrate what the coach does at various stages and choice points.

Somatech Pharmaceuticals is a world-leading healthcare company. Headquartered in Basel, Switzerland, the company has established itself as a pioneer in innovative medicines, with particular strengths in oncology, immunology, neuroscience and cardiovascular treatments. With operations in over 155 countries and approximately 105,000 employees worldwide, Somatech combines global reach with cutting-edge scientific research to address some of the world's most challenging medical conditions.

In recent years, Somatech has been navigating a significant strategic transformation, shifting from a diversified healthcare conglomerate to a focused innovative medicines company. This transition has involved divesting its generics division, Sandoz, streamlining operations and doubling down on breakthrough therapies. The company has placed particular emphasis on advanced therapeutic platforms, including cell and gene therapies, which promise to revolutionise treatments for previously intractable diseases.

The Current Challenge: The Neurocell Project

At the heart of the leadership team's current tensions lies the Neurocell project, a promising novel therapy for neurodegenerative diseases that has shown exceptional results in early clinical trials. Neurocell represents a potential game-changer in an area where treatment options have been notoriously limited. However, the project has become a flashpoint within the executive team due to competing perspectives on how to proceed with its development.

A critical decision regarding the Neurocell project has sparked significant discord among the leadership team. The debate centres on whether to advance the therapy based on promising results from a specific patient subpopulation, despite the full study not meeting its predetermined statistical endpoints. This situation has exposed different thinking styles, values, and priorities among the team members, revealing deeper tensions about how decisions should be made at Somatech.

The stakes are exceptionally high. For patients suffering from neurodegenerative conditions, Neurocell could represent a lifeline. For Somatech, it could mean a multi-million-dollar market opportunity and scientific prestige. Yet the path forward involves complex trade-offs between speed to market, scientific rigour, regulatory considerations and commercial imperatives.

The Leadership Team

Diane Marshall, CEO

Diane ascended to the CEO position three years ago after heading the company's European operations. With a background in both pharmaceutical sciences and business administration, she has cultivated a reputation for balancing scientific integrity with commercial acumen. Diane's leadership style emphasises clear decision-making and accountability, though the current Neurocell situation has tested her ability to align her executive team behind a unified approach. She feels increasing pressure from the board to demonstrate that Somatech can efficiently translate scientific discoveries into marketable medicines without sacrificing the company's standards.

Dr. Robert Chen, Chief Scientific Officer

Robert joined Somatech six months ago from a competitor, where he led several successful drug development programmes. His appointment as CSO, creating a new layer of scientific leadership above existing research heads, was part of Diane's strategy to accelerate innovation. Robert possesses profound scientific expertise coupled with an entrepreneurial mindset that embraces calculated risk. He has become the primary advocate for advancing Neurocell based on the promising subgroup analysis, arguing that mechanistic understanding sometimes precedes statistical validation. His relatively recent arrival means he's still establishing trust within the organisation.

Dr. Alisha Patel, Head of Research

Alisha has spent 15 years at Somatech, rising through the research organisation to lead the entire R&D function until Robert's appointment created a new reporting layer. With a background in molecular biology and a reputation for methodological rigour, she has helped establish Somatech's scientific credibility through adherence to robust research practices. Alisha has expressed significant concerns about the statistical validity of the Neurocell subgroup analysis, arguing that proceeding without more data could undermine the company's scientific integrity. The reorganisation that placed her under Robert has created some natural tension in their working relationship.

Emma Lawson, Head of Commercial Operations

Emma brings extensive experience from consumer healthcare before joining Somatech four years ago. Known for her market insights and customer-centric perspective, she leads the company's commercial strategy and operations. Emma sees tremendous market potential in Neurocell but is concerned about the timeline implications of additional studies. She often finds herself mediating between scientific and financial perspectives, trying to find pragmatic paths forward that serve multiple stakeholders. Her natural tendency is to seek harmony, sometimes at the expense of her own clear position.

Vincent Torres, Chief Financial Officer

Vincent has been with Somatech for eight years, with previous experience in several pharmaceutical and technology companies. His analytical mind excels at modelling complex financial scenarios and making capital allocation decisions. Vincent approaches the Neurocell decision primarily through the lens of investment returns and opportunity costs, questioning whether additional studies would deliver sufficient value given the resources required. He tends to remain emotionally detached during heated discussions, which can sometimes be perceived as disengagement from the human implications of decisions.

Michael Okafor, Head of Regulatory Affairs

Michael joined Somatech after a 12-year government career, giving him unique insight into regulatory thinking. His role involves navigating the increasingly complex global regulatory environment while advancing Somatech's innovation agenda. Regarding Neurocell, Michael has raised important questions about whether regulators would accept the subgroup analysis as sufficient for approval, cautioning against assumptions about regulatory flexibility. His regulatory expertise is highly respected, but he sometimes feels that his perspective is brought in too late in decision-making processes.

The Organisational Context

The leadership team's dynamics reflect broader tensions within Somatech as it evolves. The company was founded on scientific excellence, but faces increasing pressure to demonstrate commercial agility in a rapidly changing healthcare landscape. The recent reorganisation that created Robert's CSO role above Alisha's research position was designed to accelerate innovation but has created new coordination challenges.

Somatech's culture has traditionally emphasised methodical, evidence-based decision-making. However, the emergence of faster-moving competitors and the potential of breakthrough therapies have created internal debate about when to move quickly despite incomplete information. This tension between thorough validation and speedy innovation lies at the heart of the current leadership challenge.

The board expects the executive team to resolve the Neurocell situation decisively while maintaining both scientific credibility and commercial momentum – a balance that has proved elusive in their discussions thus far. How they navigate this decision will not only determine Neurocell's fate but also set precedents for how Somatech approaches similar situations in its pipeline, potentially reshaping the company's identity in the process.

Chapter 10

Existential Team Coaching –
Authentic Leadership

The executive conference room at Somatech Pharmaceuticals' research headquarters remained silent for a moment after Dr. Elise Johansen, the existential team coach, posed her opening question. The six members of the senior leadership team exchanged glances across the polished walnut table, the floor-to-ceiling windows offering a panoramic view of the campus that seemed to underscore the expansiveness of the question she had just asked.

"What does it mean to lead with authenticity when faced with impossible choices?" Elise had asked. "Because that's what the Neurocell situation has revealed – not just a disagreement about data, but a fundamental question about who you are as leaders and what Somatech truly stands for."

Robert Chen, the newly appointed Chief Scientific Officer, was the first to respond. "Authenticity would have been acknowledging the complexity of the data rather than reducing it to a binary go/no-go decision. The sub-analysis showed promise in a specific population that deserved consideration."

"The data wasn't statistically significant," Dr. Alisha Patel, Head of Research, countered, her voice controlled but betraying underlying frustration. "My authentic scientific judgment said Neurocell didn't meet our criteria. But somehow, that wasn't respected in what went to the board."

Elise nodded, taking in both perspectives without judgement. "I'm hearing that authenticity means different things to each of you in this context. For Robert, it means honouring complexity and potential, even if still emerging. For Alisha, it means maintaining scientific rigor and established standards." She paused. "Both are valid expressions of what matters to you as leaders."

Emma Lawson, Head of Commercial Operations, shifted in her chair. "The issue isn't just about scientific interpretation. It's about how we made a fragmented decision that confused the board and undermined our credibility. That feels like a failure of authentic leadership to me."

"Say more about that," Elise encouraged.

"Authentic leadership isn't just about expressing individual viewpoints," Emma elaborated. "It's about finding a way to act with integrity as a collective body, especially when we disagree. We didn't do that with Neurocell."

DOI: 10.4324/9781003594215-14

Vincent Torres, Chief Financial Officer, leaned forward. "Emma's right. We each advocated for our functional perspective, but nobody took responsibility for the whole. That's the authenticity gap I see – between how we present ourselves as a unified leadership team and how we actually function when tensions arise."

Diane Marshall, the CEO, who had been listening intently, spoke with unexpected candour. "I think this touches on something deeper than just the Neurocell decision. Since the reorganisation, we've been struggling with fundamental questions about our identity and purpose. Are we primarily scientists who happen to run a business, or business people who happen to work in science?"

Michael Okafor, Head of Regulatory Affairs, nodded. "That tension has always existed, but it feels more acute now. And it places each of us in a dilemma about how to authentically fulfil our roles when those roles themselves contain inherent contradictions."

Elise took a moment to reflect on what she was hearing. "What's emerging here is fascinating. You're describing not just a breakdown in decision-making but a confrontation with some of the fundamental tensions inherent in your work – tensions between scientific rigor and commercial possibility, between individual expertise and collective responsibility, between different visions of what Somatech fundamentally is." She continued, "From an existential perspective, these tensions aren't problems to be solved once and for all but rather defining aspects of your situation that must be confronted authentically. The question becomes not how to eliminate these tensions, but how to engage with them in a way that honours what matters most to each of you and to Somatech as a whole."

Robert shifted uncomfortably. "That sounds abstract. We still need to make concrete decisions about projects like Neurocell."

"Absolutely," Elise agreed. "But perhaps those concrete decisions would be approached differently if you first engaged with the deeper questions at play. For instance, what does it mean for each of you to lead authentically within an organisation that must simultaneously honour scientific integrity and commercial success? How do you make choices that reflect both realities rather than privileging one over the other?"

Alisha, who had been listening with growing interest, spoke up. "I came to Somatech because I believed in developing medicines based on sound science. That's what gives my work meaning. When I feel that scientific rigor is being compromised for commercial expedience, it creates not just disagreement but a kind of . . . existential distress. Like I'm betraying what matters most to me."

"And I joined to help get life-changing medicines to patients," Emma countered. "When promising treatments get delayed or abandoned because of overly conservative interpretations of data, I feel a similar distress – like we're betraying patients who are waiting for solutions."

Elise nodded. "You're both describing clearly what authentic leadership means – aligning your actions with your core values and sense of purpose. The challenge is that your genuine concerns sometimes place you at odds with each other."

"So, whose authenticity wins?" Robert asked, with a hint of scepticism in his voice.

"That's precisely the question," Elise replied. "And it's one that existential thinking would suggest can't be answered through abstract principles alone but must be engaged with in each specific situation. What does it mean to make an authentic choice together, one that honours the complexity of your shared purpose rather than reducing it to one dimension?"

Diane leaned forward. "I think that's where we've been failing. We've been treating these tensions as either/or questions that have to be resolved in favour of one perspective, rather than both/and challenges that require us to hold complexity together."

"Yes," Elise says. "And that approach reflects a deeper existential theme – a discomfort with ambiguity and a desire for certainty in situations where certainty may not be possible. The reality of your work involves inherent tensions and competing values that can't be eliminated, only engaged with – authentically."

Vincent, who had been thoughtfully observing, spoke up. "This reminds me of why I found the reorganisation so challenging. My role used to be clearly defined – I was the financial gatekeeper. Now I'm expected to be both a steward of resources and an enabler of innovation. Those aspects sometimes conflict, and I've struggled to find an effective way to embody both."

"You're describing a fundamental existential challenge – how to create meaning and authenticity within roles that contain inherent contradictions," Elise observed. "Rather than seeing this as a failure, perhaps it's an invitation to develop a more nuanced understanding of your role and purpose."

Michael nodded. "In Regulatory, we live this tension every day – between ensuring safety and enabling access. We've learned that authentic leadership means acknowledging both imperatives rather than pretending the tension doesn't exist."

"Michael, you've touched on something important," Elise said. "Authenticity doesn't mean absence of tension or contradiction. It means engaging openly with those tensions rather than denying them or pretending they can be permanently resolved." She continued, "Let's bring this back to Neurocell. What would it have looked like to engage authentically with the tensions inherent in that decision, rather than allowing them to fracture your team?"

The room fell silent as they considered the question. Finally, Alisha spoke. "We could have acknowledged that both scientific rigor and potential patient benefit matter, rather than positioning them as opposing considerations. We could have presented the board with a unified assessment that captured the complexity rather than fragmented messages."

"And we could have been more transparent about our different perspectives while still taking collective responsibility for a recommendation," Robert added, surprising others with his shift in tone.

"What I'm hearing," Elise observed, "is a vision of authentic leadership that doesn't require unanimous agreement but does require honest engagement with complexity and collective – responsibility for decisions, even amid disagreement."

Diane nodded thoughtfully. "That feels right. Authenticity isn't about everyone agreeing – it's about creating a space where different perspectives can be fully expressed and genuinely considered before we make decisions that we all then support."

"And perhaps more fundamentally," Elise suggested, "it's about acknowledging that the tensions you face – between science and commerce, between individual expertise and collective judgment, between certainty and possibility – aren't failures of your organisation but essential aspects of the complex work you do together."

Emma, who had been quiet for some time, spoke up. "I think there's something else here too. When Robert shared the additional data with the board, I felt betrayed – like my voice didn't matter. Similarly, Robert probably felt dismissed when his concerns about the sub-analysis weren't fully considered in our initial recommendation."

Robert nodded in acknowledgement.

"So, there's an interpersonal dimension to authenticity as well," Elise noted. "It involves not just alignment with your own values but genuine recognition of others as fellow meaning-makers whose perspectives deserve engagement, even when they differ from your own."

"That's what was missing with Neurocell," Vincent realised. "Not agreement, but authentic engagement across our differences."

As the session continued, Elise guided the team towards exploring how they might create structures and practices that would support more authentic engagement with the tensions inherent in their work. They discussed how decision-making processes could be redesigned to encourage fuller expression of competing perspectives before reaching collective judgements. They explored how their roles could be reconceived to explicitly acknowledge rather than deny the contradictions each leader faced.

"What I'm observing," Elise noted towards the end of their time together, "is a shift from seeing your tensions and disagreements as problems to be eliminated towards viewing them as invitations to more authentic leadership – leadership that engages openly with complexity rather than seeking premature resolution." She continued, "From an existential perspective, the anxieties that arise when facing difficult decisions like Neurocell aren't distractions from your work but central to it. The question isn't how to eliminate that anxiety but how to face it together with courage and authenticity rather than allowing it to fracture your team."

As they prepared to conclude, Diane spoke with renewed clarity. "I think what we're discovering is that authentic leadership for us means holding seemingly contradictory truths simultaneously – that we are both a scientific organisation and a commercial enterprise, that decisions require both individual expertise and collective judgment, that success means both rigorous standards and openness to unexpected possibilities."

"Yes," Elise said. "And recognising that navigating those tensions isn't a distraction from your purpose but the very essence of it."

As the session ended, there was a palpable shift in the atmosphere. The tension hadn't disappeared – indeed, the existential approach hadn't sought to eliminate it – but there was a new quality to their interactions, a willingness to engage with complexity rather than reduce it to simplistic oppositions.

Robert and Alisha, whose conflict had been at the centre of the Neurocell situation, paused near the door to continue their conversation, no longer positioning themselves as opponents but as colleagues struggling with authentic engagement across genuine differences. Emma and Vincent discussed how they might restructure upcoming pipeline reviews to better honour both commercial and financial perspectives. Michael engaged directly with Diane about how to communicate this evolving understanding of authentic leadership to their respective teams.

The path forward wasn't marked by certainty or permanent resolution of tensions. But in acknowledging and engaging with those tensions authentically, the team had discovered a more meaningful and honest way of working together – one that honoured the complex reality of their shared purpose rather than reducing it to simplistic choices between competing values.

Analysing the Session

This fictional team coaching session illustrates several core principles and techniques of existential coaching applied in a team context. Let's analyse what transpired from an existential coaching perspective:

1. Authenticity – Authenticity is the central theme of the coaching session and includes multiple perspectives on authenticity.

   Each team member initially defines authenticity differently – for Robert, it means "honouring complexity"; for Alisha, it means "maintaining scientific rigor"; and for Emma, it involves "acting with integrity as a collective body." This illustrates the existential view that authenticity is not a fixed state but an ongoing process of aligning actions with values. The coach helps the team recognise that authentic leadership doesn't mean eliminating tensions or contradictions but engaging openly with them. As Elise states, "Authenticity doesn't mean absence of tension or contradiction. It means engaging openly with those tensions rather than denying them." Alisha's "existential distress" when scientific rigour seems compromised and Emma's similar feeling when promising treatments are delayed illustrate important signals that actions are misaligned with core values.

2. Freedom and Responsibility – the existential theme of freedom and responsibility runs throughout the session.

   Authentic choice: Elise frames the Neurocell situation not merely as a decision-making failure but also as a question about what it means to lead with authenticity when faced with impossible choices. This reframes the issue in terms of existential freedom and the responsibility that comes with it. The team recognises their failure to take collective responsibility for decisions, with Vincent observing that "nobody took responsibility for the whole." This reflects the existential understanding that freedom and responsibility are intertwined. The team confronts the reality that leadership decisions must be made without complete certainty, reflecting the existential view that human existence can involve making choices under conditions of uncertainty and ambiguity. The session moves the team towards what existentialists might call "response-ability" – the capacity to respond authentically to complex situations rather than defaulting to pre-determined patterns or avoiding difficult choices.

3. Meaning and Purpose – the exploration of meaning and purpose is evident throughout.

   Team members articulate what gives their work meaning – Alisha came to Somatech "because I believed in developing medicines based on sound science," while Emma "joined to help get life-changing medicines to patients." These statements reflect the existential focus on how humans create meaning through a commitment to action. The team grapples with fundamental questions about organisational identity: "Are we primarily scientists who happen to run a business, or business people who happen to work in science?" This reflects the existential understanding that purpose is not given but created through choice and commitment. Rather than choosing between scientific and commercial identities, the team moves towards integrating these as dual aspects of a more complex purpose. Diane articulates this when she says authentic leadership means "holding seemingly contradictory truths simultaneously."

   Finally, the session reframes the tensions the team faces not as problems to be eliminated but as essential aspects of meaningful work – what Elise calls "invitations to more authentic leadership."

4. Anxiety – the existential understanding of anxiety as inherent in human existence is also addressed.

   Elise explicitly states that "the anxieties that arise when facing difficult decisions like Neurocell aren't distractions from your work but central to it," reflecting the existential view that anxiety is not pathological but a natural response to freedom and uncertainty. The team's fragmented communication to the board represents what existentialists might call "bad faith" – inauthentic actions taken to avoid the anxiety of confronting complex choices and taking full responsibility. The coach encourages the team to face anxiety "with courage and authenticity rather than allowing it to fracture your team," emphasising that courage involves facing uncertainty rather than eliminating it. Elise names the "deeper existential theme – our discomfort with ambiguity and our desire for certainty in situations where certainty may not be possible," helping the team recognise how this discomfort influences their decision-making.

5. Paradox – the session works extensively with existential paradoxes and polarities.

   Diane recognises they've been treating tensions as "either/or questions" when they need to approach them as "both/and challenges that require us to hold complexity together." This reflects the existential embrace of paradox rather than forced resolution. The team explores how to integrate seemingly opposed values – scientific rigour and commercial success, individual expertise and collective judgement, certainty and possibility – without eliminating the tension between them. Vincent's struggle with being "both a steward of resources and an enabler of innovation" illustrates the existential challenge of creating unified meaning from seemingly contradictory elements. Though not explicitly named, the session demonstrates what existential and Gestalt practitioners call the "paradoxical theory of change" – that authentic change comes not from trying to be something different but from fully acknowledging what one is.

The Coach's Existential Approach

Elise demonstrates several key aspects of the existential coaching technique.

- Phenomenological stance: She begins with the team's lived experience of the Neurocell situation rather than imposing external frameworks or solutions.
- Philosophical exploration: She introduces existential concepts like authenticity, meaning and anxiety in practical, applied ways that illuminate the team's experience rather than as abstract philosophical ideas.
- Embracing tension: Rather than trying to resolve tensions or eliminate anxiety, she helps the team engage more fully with these as essential aspects of their situation.
- Focus on choice and meaning: She consistently directs attention to how team members are creating meaning through their choices rather than searching for external validation or predetermined answers.
- Authenticity: She emphasises not just individual authenticity but also how authenticity functions in relationships, helping the team see each other as "fellow meaning-makers whose perspectives deserve engagement."

Key Shifts in the Session

Several pivotal moments in the session represent significant shifts in the team's awareness.

From technical to existential framing. The initial reframing of the Neurocell situation from a technical disagreement to a question of authentic leadership sets the tone for deeper exploration. From individual to collective authenticity. The recognition that authenticity involves not just individual expression but collective responsibility for decisions even amid disagreement. From problem-solving to meaning-making. The shift from seeing tensions as problems to be solved to viewing them as essential aspects of meaningful work. From either/or to both/and thinking. Diane's recognition that they've been treating complex issues as binary choices rather than paradoxes to be embraced. From avoiding to engaging with anxiety. The team's growing willingness to face the anxiety inherent in complex choices rather than fragmenting to avoid it.

Outcomes and Emerging Directions

The session leads to several important outcomes consistent with existential coaching.

1. Greater authenticity: Team members develop a more nuanced understanding of authenticity that includes both personal values and collective responsibility.
2. Meaningful engagement with anxiety: Rather than seeking to eliminate tension, the team begins to see how engaging with tension can create more meaningful and effective leadership.
3. Courage in uncertainty: The team develops a greater capacity to face uncertainty with courage rather than retreating to the false security of oversimplification.
4. Inter-subjective recognition: Team members begin to recognise each other more fully as fellow meaning-makers with legitimate, though different, perspectives.
5. Integration rather than fragmentation: The session ends with a more integrated approach to leadership that holds scientific and commercial realities together rather than splitting them apart.

Unlike approaches that might focus primarily on improving communication techniques or clarifying decision processes, the existential coaching approach addresses the deeper questions of meaning, authenticity, freedom and responsibility that underlie the team's challenges. It doesn't provide simple solutions but helps the team develop a more meaningful and authentic way of engaging with the inherent tensions and contradictions of their work.

The session demonstrates how existential coaching in a team context isn't about eliminating conflicts or tensions but about helping the team engage with these in more authentic and meaningful ways. Rather than pursuing artificial harmony, the existential approach fosters the courage to face complexity together – acknowledging both scientific and commercial realities, both individual expertise and collective responsibility and both certainty and possibility as essential aspects of authentic leadership.

Chapter 11

Systems Psychodynamic Team Coaching – *Fault Lines*

The executive conference room at Somatech Pharmaceuticals' research headquarters was designed to impress, with floor-to-ceiling windows overlooking the campus grounds and a massive oval table of polished walnut. Today, however, the room's grandeur seemed at odds with the palpable tension that hung in the air as the senior leadership team assembled.

Dr. Maya Singh, the systems-psychodynamic coach who had been working with the team for three months, observed the executives as they entered. Their movements, seating choices and initial interactions were data-unconscious communications about the team's current state.

Robert Chen, the newly appointed Chief Scientific Officer, entered first, selecting a seat at the far end of the table with a clear view of the door. Emma Lawson, Head of Commercial Operations, and Vincent Torres, Chief Financial Officer, arrived together but separated to sit on opposite sides of the table. Dr. Alisha Patel, Head of Research, deliberately placed herself between Robert and the empty chair at the head of the table, where CEO Diane Marshall would sit. Michael Okafor, Head of Regulatory Affairs, chose a seat somewhat removed from the others, his expression carefully neutral.

The team members exchanged perfunctory greetings, their usual pre-meeting banter noticeably absent. When Diane entered, the subtle straightening of postures and redirection of attention were immediate. She took her place at the head of the table with a tight smile.

"Thank you all for making time for this session," Maya began once everyone had settled. "As we discussed in our previous meeting, today we're going to explore some of the dynamics that might be affecting how you function as a leadership team, particularly around decision-making and collaboration."

Vincent cleared his throat. "Before we dive into the abstract, I think we should acknowledge the elephant in the room. The Neurocell project decision last week was a disaster. Three different messages went to the board, and now they're questioning our collective judgment."

A visible ripple of tension moved around the table. Emma's shoulders stiffened, while Robert's expression hardened into something defensive.

DOI: 10.4324/9781003594215-15

"That's a significant concern," Maya acknowledged. "Perhaps we could use the Neurocell situation as a way to understand what's happening beneath the surface in this team. Who would like to share their perspective on how that decision process unfolded?"

A weighted silence settled over the room until Diane spoke. "I'll start. The Neurocell decision should have been straightforward. We had agreed on criteria for advancing pipeline projects beyond Phase II. Neurocell didn't meet those criteria. Yet somehow, a recommendation to continue funding reached the board – directly contradicting the preliminary consensus we had reached as a team."

Robert shifted in his chair. "With respect, Diane, that 'preliminary consensus' was reached before the latest trial data sub-analysis, which showed significant promise in a specific patient population. Science evolves. Our decisions should evolve with it."

"The sub-analysis wasn't powered correctly," Alisha interjected, her voice controlled but sharp. "As I explained in the meeting, we can't base million-dollar decisions on statistically questionable results."

"And yet the board needed to hear about those results," Robert insisted. "They deserved the complete picture."

"Which they would have received," Emma said, her frustration evident, "if we had aligned on a unified message instead of you going rogue in the pre-read materials."

Maya observed the escalating tension, noting how the conversation was quickly replicating the very dynamic that had created the problem. "I'm noticing something interesting happening right now," she interjected. "The conversation has immediately moved to who was right about the science rather than the process by which you make decisions as a team. I wonder if that pattern might tell us something important."

The room fell silent as the team absorbed her observation.

"Let me suggest a different approach," Maya continued. "Rather than debating the merits of Neurocell itself, I'm curious about what this situation might represent in your system. What deeper patterns or tensions might be playing out through this particular decision?"

Michael, who had remained silent until now, spoke up. "There's been tension since Robert joined six months ago. Not because of Robert personally," he added quickly, glancing at his colleague, "but because his role represents a shift in how we approach R&D. The creation of the CSO position above existing research heads was always going to create friction."

Alisha's jaw tightened, but she remained silent.

"That's a helpful observation, Michael," Maya said. "I'm wondering how others experience this structural change and what it might mean for how authority and expertise are distributed in the organisation."

"It means we have unclear decision rights," Alisha said finally, her voice careful but carrying an undercurrent of resentment. "I used to report directly to Diane. Now I report to Robert, but Diane still expects me to bring research concerns directly to her attention. When the three of us have different views on a project like Neurocell, whose voice matters most?"

Robert leaned forward. "Science should matter most. Data should matter most."

"But science doesn't speak for itself," Alisha countered. "It's interpreted. And in this case, your interpretation contradicted mine – despite my team having worked on this molecule for four years."

Maya noticed that the conversation was exposing a fundamental tension regarding authority and expertise. "I'm hearing something about how expertise is valued and how decisions get made when there are competing expert views. This seems to go beyond Neurocell to something more fundamental about how you function as a system."

Vincent, who had been watching the exchange with growing impatience, cut in. "Let's be honest here. This isn't just about organisational structure or decision rights. There's a deeper divide in this room about our purpose as a company. Are we primarily a scientific organisation that happens to sell products, or a commercial enterprise that happens to use science? That tension has always existed, but it's escalated since we reorganised."

A current of recognition passed through the room – Vincent had named something that usually remained beneath the surface.

"That's a significant observation," Maya acknowledged. "I'm curious how each of you experiences that tension between scientific and commercial identities. And perhaps more importantly, how that tension gets managed – or not managed – in your collective decision-making."

Diane, who had been listening intently, spoke with unexpected candour. "When I became CEO three years ago, I promised the board I would balance our scientific heritage with commercial discipline. But lately, I feel like I'm constantly mediating between competing worldviews." Her voice carried a note of fatigue that seemed to surprise everyone. "The reorganisation was meant to strengthen both sides, not force them into opposition."

"Yet here we are," Emma said softly. "Living that opposition every day."

Maya observed how Diane's vulnerability had shifted something in the room. "I wonder if this tension between scientific and commercial identities is something this team is specifically holding for the entire organisation. In systems-psychodynamic terms, key groups often carry particular tensions or polarities on behalf of the larger system."

"What do you mean?" Robert asked, genuinely curious.

"Organisations often develop unconscious patterns where certain groups become repositories for particular values or perspectives," Maya explained. "In this case, this leadership team may be embodying a tension that exists throughout the company – the dual identity as both a scientific and commercial enterprise. Rather than this tension being worked with constructively across the organisation, it becomes concentrated and polarised at the leadership level."

"So, we're acting out the organisation's identity crisis?" Alisha asked, with a hint of sceptical humour.

"In a sense, yes," Maya replied. "But I think it's more that you're trying to hold both realities simultaneously, which is incredibly difficult when these different aspects of organisational identity are seen as opposing forces rather than complementary ones."

Michael, who had been thoughtfully observing, spoke up. "That resonates with my experience in Regulatory. We constantly navigate between scientific rigor and commercial timelines. But we don't see them as opposing forces – we see them as different dimensions of the same mission. Perhaps at the leadership level, we've lost that integration."

A thoughtful silence followed this observation.

"I'd like to try something," Maya suggested. "Rather than seeing the scientific and commercial perspectives as competing, what if we viewed them as two essential aspects of your collective role as a leadership team? Not Robert versus Emma, or Research versus Commercial, but all of you collectively holding both the scientific integrity and commercial success of Somatech?"

She continued, "What might it look like if, instead of each of you primarily advocating for your functional perspective, you all held responsibility for both the scientific and commercial futures of the organisation?"

Vincent frowned. "That sounds good in theory, but practically speaking, we have different expertise. I can't evaluate clinical trial data the way Alisha and Robert can."

"I'm not suggesting everyone becomes an expert in everything," Maya clarified. "I'm wondering if there's a way to integrate these perspectives at the leadership team level, even as you maintain your functional expertise. To create a space where these tensions can be worked with productively rather than becoming polarised."

Diane nodded slowly. "That was the original intent of reorganising – to strengthen both dimensions. But somehow we've ended up more siloed, not less."

"That's often how anxiety gets managed in organisations," Maya observed. "When facing complex challenges, there's a tendency to retreat to familiar territory – to strengthen boundaries rather than work across them. The question is whether that pattern is serving your collective purpose."

Robert, who had been listening intently, also spoke with unexpected vulnerability. "When I took this role, I was excited about bridging the gap between pure research and clinical development. But honestly, I've felt caught between competing expectations from day one. Alisha's team sees me as Diane's enforcer of commercial discipline, while the board expects me to accelerate our pipeline regardless of what researchers think is realistic."

Alisha looked at Robert with surprise, seeing him in a new light. "I didn't realise you felt caught in the middle too. I assumed you were brought in specifically to override research concerns in favour of faster development."

"That's not how I see my role at all," Robert replied, meeting her gaze.

Maya noted this moment of genuine connection. "This is important. You're beginning to see beyond the surface conflicts to the systemic pressures shaping each of your roles. Robert isn't just acting from personal preference when he pushes certain projects forward – he's responding to pressures and expectations built into his role in this system."

She turned to address the whole team. "Each of you is subject to different pressures and expectations based on your position in the structure. Understanding those systemic influences – rather than just seeing conflicts as personality clashes or power struggles – creates the possibility for different kinds of conversations."

Emma, who had been unusually quiet, spoke up. "This reminds me of when I first joined from outside the industry. I was shocked by how researchers viewed commercial colleagues as somehow less committed to patients. As if making medicines available and affordable wasn't as important as discovering them."

"And commercial sometimes acts like research is an expensive hobby rather than the lifeblood of our future," Alisha countered with less heat than before.

Diane leaned forward. "This gets at something fundamental about our identity as an organisation. We talk about being 'science-led and patient-focused,' but we haven't really worked through what that means when tough decisions need to be made."

"Or who gets to decide what 'science-led' means in practice," Vincent added.

Maya nodded. "You're touching on something critical about authority in the system – not just formal authority from the organisational chart, but psychological authority: whose expertise is trusted, whose interpretation matters most, who feels empowered to speak on behalf of 'science' or 'patients' or 'shareholders.'"

She paused to let that sink in. "The Neurocell situation isn't just about one project or one miscommunication. It's revealing fundamental questions about how this team and this organisation manages tensions inherent in your work. How do you integrate scientific and commercial realities? How do you distribute authority among experts? How do you make decisions when legitimate perspectives conflict?"

The room fell silent as the team absorbed the shift from seeing their conflict as a communication breakdown to recognising it as a manifestation of deeper systemic dynamics.

After a moment, Maya continued. "I'm wondering if we might use our remaining time to explore what it would mean to hold these tensions differently – not by eliminating them, but by creating structures and processes that allow them to be worked with productively."

Diane straightened in her chair, a new determination in her posture. "That's exactly what we need. Not pretending the tensions don't exist but finding better ways to work with them." She looked around the table. "I realise now I've sometimes tried to resolve tensions by executive decision when what was needed was a deeper exploration of competing perspectives."

"And I've sometimes advocated for my area without fully engaging with others' legitimate concerns," Emma acknowledged.

"We all have," Michael added. "It's natural to protect your functional territory. The question is whether we can find ways to transcend those boundaries when needed without erasing them entirely."

For the remainder of the session, the team began exploring specific changes to how they structured decision-making processes, particularly for complex, cross-functional issues like pipeline investments. The conversation wasn't easy – moments of tension and disagreement still emerged – but there was a different quality to the engagement. Rather than positioning themselves as opponents, team members began to recognise their shared responsibility for holding the organisation's complex identity.

As the session drew to a close, Maya reflected on what she had observed. "Today, you've begun to see your conflicts not just as interpersonal issues but as expressions of deeper systemic dynamics. That shift opens new possibilities for how you work together." She continued, "The tensions between scientific integrity and commercial success, between different forms of expertise, between autonomy and alignment – these aren't problems to solve once and for all. They're polarities to be managed continuously. The question is whether you can create conditions where these tensions generate creative energy rather than destructive conflict."

Diane nodded. "This won't be resolved in one session. But I think we've at least begun to see the real nature of our challenge." She looked around at her team. "And perhaps to see each other more fully as well."

As the executives gathered their materials to leave, Maya noticed subtle but significant changes in how they moved and interacted. Robert and Alisha exited together, continuing a conversation that had begun during the session. Emma and Vincent, who had arrived together but sat apart, now stood side by side, reviewing notes. Michael engaged directly with Diane rather than maintaining his usual careful distance.

These small shifts in the team's spatial relationships mirrored the psychological movement that had begun – from rigid polarisation towards the possibility of more fluid, integrated functioning. The fault lines remained, but they had begun to be acknowledged not as failures but as essential features of the complex system they were collectively responsible for leading.

Analysing the Session

This fictional team coaching session illustrates several core principles and techniques of systems-psychodynamic team coaching. Let's analyse what transpired from a systems-psychodynamic perspective.

The Organisation as a Container for Anxiety

The session reveals how the leadership team functions as a container for organisational anxiety in several ways.

The Neurocell project decision represents a focal point for anxiety about the company's scientific integrity, commercial success and future. Rather than being contained and worked with productively, this anxiety manifested in fragmented communications and competing messages to the board. The team is also holding anxiety about Somatech's dual identity as both a scientific and commercial enterprise. Vincent names this explicitly: "There's a deeper divide in this room about our purpose as a company." The reorganisation and creation of the CSO role has created structural anxiety about authority, expertise and decision rights, which Alisha articulates when she says, "When the three of us have different views on a project like Neurocell, whose voice matters most?" Maya helps the team recognise how these anxieties are influencing their behaviour, not just as individual psychological reactions but also as systemic patterns that affect how the organisation functions.

The coaching session also highlights several social defences that have developed within the team as a direct result of all this anxiety. The most prominent defence we see is *Splitting*, in this case between the company's "scientific" and "commercial" identities, embodied in the polarisation between different team members. Rather than integrating these perspectives, the team have split them into competing camps. There is also a case of siloing that Diane observes with her comment that after the reorganisation, the company has ended up "more siloed, not less," reflecting how the team has managed anxiety by retreating to functional territories with clearer boundaries. We also see clear evidence of *Projection*. Research projects scientific purity onto itself while projecting compromise onto commercial; commercial projects practical reality onto itself while projecting impractical idealism onto research. Emma names this when she mentions how "researchers viewed commercial colleagues as somehow less committed to patients." Finally, we see clear *Displacement* activity. The conflict over Neurocell serves as a displacement, where deeper anxieties about organisational identity and authority are channelled into debate about a specific project rather than addressing the underlying tensions.

Maya helps the team recognise these various defences not as personal failings but as systemic responses to anxiety that have emerged unconsciously to protect them from having to directly confront difficult tensions and contradictions.

The Primary Task and Anti-Task

The session reveals confusion about the primary task of both the organisation and the leadership team.

There are competing definitions of purpose. Vincent explicitly names the tension between understanding Somatech as "primarily a scientific organisation that happens to sell products, or a commercial enterprise that happens to use science." There is also leadership task confusion. Ambiguity exists about whether the leadership team's primary task is to advocate for functional perspectives or to integrate these perspectives on behalf of the organisation as a whole. We also see anti-task behaviour. The team's fragmented communication to the board represents anti-task behaviour – that is, actions that appear to serve the organisation's mission but actually undermine it by creating confusion and eroding trust.

Maya helps the team reconnect with a more integrated understanding of their primary task, suggesting "all of you collectively holding both the scientific integrity and commercial success of Somatech" rather than seeing these as competing priorities.

Role and Authority

Role and authority issues are central to most team dynamics, and dysfunctions can be seen in this example.

We see clear role confusion. Robert's experience of being "caught between competing expectations" highlights how role confusion contributes to system dysfunction. His formal role (CSO) also carries ambiguous psychological expectations. Alisha's comment about unclear reporting lines ("I used to report directly to Diane. Now I report to Robert, but Diane still expects me to bring research concerns directly to her attention") also reveals unclear authority boundaries. The tension between different forms of expertise authority (scientific, commercial and financial) raises questions about whose knowledge should take precedence in different contexts – what Maya refers to as "psychological authority."

Maya helps the team see how each member's behaviour is shaped by their role in the system, not just their personal preferences or personality, noting that "Robert isn't just acting from personal preference . . . he's responding to pressures and expectations built into his role in this system." Ultimately, the coaching helps team members distinguish between the person, the role and the system, creating space to examine how roles are taken up rather than just focusing on individual behaviours.

Boundary Management

Several boundary issues also emerge during the coaching.

The reorganisation has created new structural boundaries between functions that the team is clearly struggling to navigate effectively. In addition, the team has created rigid psychological boundaries between scientific and commercial identities rather than managing the interface between these domains. The fragmented communication to the board represents a failure to manage information boundaries effectively. The coaching helps the team recognise these boundary issues and begin exploring how to make them more permeable without eliminating necessary distinctions.

The Coach's Systems-Psychodynamic Approach

Maya demonstrates the systems-psychodynamic emphasis on working with what emerges in the present moment through various approaches, which focuses the group on present experience and helps move the work beyond abstract discussion to lived exploration of the team's dynamics.

- *Physical data*: She observes and utilises information about how team members enter, arrange themselves and interact in the room as data about the system.
- *In-the-moment dynamics*: When the team immediately begins debating the merits of the Neurocell decision, Maya points out that this replicates the very pattern that created the problem, using the here-and-now interaction as a window into systemic patterns.
- *Emotional climate*: She attends to shifts in the emotional atmosphere of the room, such as the impact of Diane's unexpected vulnerability.

Throughout the session, Maya consistently offers interpretations that link individual behaviours to underlying systemic patterns. For example:

- *Polarities as systemic*: Maya frames the scientific/commercial tension not as a personality clash but as a polarity that exists throughout the organisation that the leadership team is specifically "holding for the entire organisation."
- *Role behaviour as systemic*: She also helps team members see each other's actions as shaped by their positions in the system rather than merely as personal choices.
- *Conflicts as systemic information*: The Neurocell conflict is reframed as important information about deeper systemic dynamics rather than simply a communication failure to be fixed.

These interpretations help shift the team from blaming individuals to understanding patterns that help create new possibilities for interventions at the system level. Maya also demonstrates several other key elements of the systems-psychodynamic technique.

- *Containing anxiety*: She creates a psychological container where difficult tensions can be acknowledged and explored rather than avoided or acted out.
- Working with defences: Rather than confronting defences directly, she helps the team recognise their defensive patterns and the anxieties they manage, treating them as data about the system.
- *Using self as instrument*: She notices and utilises her own reactions and observations as information about the system, such as when she points out the immediate replication of conflictual patterns in the room.
- *Linking individual to system*: She consistently connects individual behaviours and experiences to larger systemic patterns and organisational dynamics.
- *Working with the unconscious*: She helps bring unconscious assumptions and patterns into awareness, such as the unspoken beliefs about what it means to be "science-led."

Key Turning Points in the Session

Several pivotal moments represent significant shifts in the team's awareness. Vincent articulates the fundamental identity question ("Are we primarily a scientific organisation that happens to sell products, or a commercial enterprise that happens to use science?"), and in doing so, he brings a previously unconscious dynamic into explicit awareness. The CEO's admission of fatigue from constantly mediating between competing worldviews creates a shift in the emotional climate, making it safer for others to show vulnerability. When Robert shares his experience of being "caught between competing expectations," and Alisha realises that she had misunderstood his role, and a new possibility for a relationship emerges beyond a previously rigid boundary. Michael's observation that in Regulatory they see scientific and commercial perspectives as "different dimensions of the same mission" offers the team a model for integration rather than polarisation. Finally, Maya's suggestion that their collective role involves holding both scientific and commercial realities shifts the frame from resolving tensions to managing them productively.

Outcomes and Emerging Directions

This fictional session produces several important outcomes consistent with systems-psychodynamic coaching.

1. Systemic awareness: The team develops greater awareness of how their conflicts reflect larger organisational dynamics rather than just interpersonal issues.
2. Role clarity: Members begin to understand how their roles in the system shape their perspectives and behaviours, creating more empathy and less personalisation of conflicts.
3. Integration: The team begins to see the possibilities for integrating seemingly opposed perspectives rather than remaining polarised.
4. New authority relationships: The awareness of how formal and psychological authority operate in the system opens possibilities for more effective distribution of decision rights.

Throughout the session, Maya embodies the systems-psychodynamic approach by consistently attending to unconscious dynamics, linking individual behaviours to systemic patterns and treating presenting problems (like the Neurocell conflict) as expressions of deeper organisational tensions rather than isolated incidents to be resolved.

The coaching demonstrates how systems-psychodynamic teamwork goes beyond addressing interpersonal conflicts or improving communication to engage with the fundamental anxieties, identity questions and authority dilemmas that shape organisational life. By bringing these dynamics into awareness, the session creates new possibilities for the team to function as an effective container for organisational anxiety rather than being overwhelmed by it or unconsciously acting it out.

Chapter 12

Gestalt Team Coaching – *The Space Between*

The executive conference room at Somatech Pharmaceuticals' research headquarters was designed to impress, with floor-to-ceiling windows overlooking the campus grounds. Today, however, the spacious room felt charged with a peculiar energy as the senior leadership team assembled, their movements deliberate and guarded.

Dr. Elena Vega, the Gestalt coach who had been working with the team for three months, arrived early to prepare the space. Rather than the typical boardroom arrangement, she had pushed the massive walnut table to one side and arranged chairs in a circle. As team members entered, their reactions to this unfamiliar configuration were telling – hesitations at the threshold, questioning glances and subtle adjustments to their usual professional composure.

Robert Chen, the newly appointed Chief Scientific Officer, entered first, selecting a seat with a clear sightline to the door. Emma Lawson, Head of Commercial Operations, and Vincent Torres, Chief Financial Officer, arrived together but chose seats across from each other. Dr. Alisha Patel, Head of Research, positioned herself with visible calculation, leaving an empty chair between herself and where Robert sat. Michael Okafor, Head of Regulatory Affairs, entered and paused, scanning the room before selecting a seat somewhat removed from the others. When CEO Diane Marshall arrived last, she momentarily hesitated at the circle format before taking the remaining chair.

"Welcome, everyone," Elena began once they had settled. "I'd like to start our session by simply inviting each of you to share what you're experiencing right now, in this moment – physically, emotionally, mentally – as you sit in this circle together."

The invitation was met with a charged silence. The executives exchanged glances, their usual confident demeanours momentarily suspended.

"I'm aware of feeling . . . uncomfortable," Diane finally offered, her tone measured. "This arrangement makes it impossible to hide behind laptops or paperwork. And I notice I'm sitting straighter than usual." She paused, then added with surprising candour, "I also feel exposed, somehow."

"Thank you for that awareness, Diane," Elena acknowledged. "What happens if you stay with that feeling of exposure for a moment? Is there a physical sensation that accompanies it?"

DOI: 10.4324/9781003594215-16

Diane's eyes widened slightly, unused to such direct focus on her experience. "There's a tightness across my chest. And my shoulders feel tense." She straightened, then consciously relaxed her shoulders. "It's as if I'm bracing for something."

Elena nodded, allowing space for this observation to land. "Who else is noticing something in their immediate experience?"

"I'm aware that I deliberately positioned myself with space between Robert and me," Alisha offered, gesturing to the empty chair. "And I'm feeling a knot in my stomach as I say that aloud."

Robert shifted in his chair, his gaze moving to the empty seat between them. "I notice I'm feeling . . . defensive," he acknowledged. "Even before anything has been said about the Neurocell situation. My jaw is tight, and I'm already preparing counterarguments in my head."

"I appreciate that awareness, Robert," Elena responded. "Rather than going to those counterarguments right now, can you stay with the physical sensation in your jaw? What happens when you simply notice that tension?"

Robert paused, his attention turning inward. "It's . . . intense. And familiar. I realise I've been carrying this tension for weeks, not just today."

"We all have," Emma added, leaning forward slightly. "I notice I've been holding my breath since we started, literally not breathing fully. And I'm positioned like I'm ready to jump in and mediate between different perspectives – it's physically uncomfortable but completely habitual."

As each person shared their immediate awareness, Elena guided them to notice both their physical presence and the quality of contact they were making with themselves and others. She observed aloud how some were making direct eye contact while others were looking at the floor or middle distance and how some were fully occupying their chairs while others perched at the edges.

"What's emerging here is significant," Elena noted. "Before we discuss any content about the Neurocell project decision, you're becoming aware of how you're physically and emotionally present to this situation right now. This awareness creates choices that might not otherwise be available." She continued, "I'd like to try an experiment that might help us explore what's happening in your team. Would you be willing to physically arrange yourselves in a way that represents how you've been functioning around the Neurocell decision?"

After a moment of surprised consideration, the team members nodded and stood up. Without discussion, they began moving into position. Diane placed herself centrally but slightly elevated, standing on a small platform near the window. Robert and Alisha moved to opposite sides of the room, facing away from each other. Emma positioned herself between them, facing back and forth. Vincent stood slightly behind Diane, while Michael placed himself at a distance from everyone, observing.

"Take a moment to notice this configuration," Elena invited. "What do you observe about how you've arranged yourselves?"

"We're polarised," Vincent observed immediately. "Split into opposing camps."

"I'm literally turning my back on Robert," Alisha noted, her voice carrying a hint of surprise at her own positioning.

"And I'm trying to see both sides simultaneously," Emma added, "which is physically impossible."

"I'm above the fray but not really connected to what's happening on the ground," Diane realised, looking down from her elevated position.

Elena nodded. "This physical arrangement is making visible patterns that are usually implicit. You're giving form to how you've been functioning as a team." She paused. "Notice what it feels like to stand in this configuration. What emerges for you?"

"It feels awful," Robert admitted with unexpected vulnerability. "Isolated. Like I'm just defending a position."

"I can't see everyone from where I'm standing," Diane observed. "Parts of the team are blocked from my view depending on where I focus."

Michael, who had positioned himself at a distance, spoke up. "I notice I've put myself in an observer role, not directly involved. It's safer, but also . . . disconnected."

Elena let these awareness sink in. "What might happen if you made one move – just one – to shift this configuration toward something that would better support your collective work on Neurocell?"

After a thoughtful pause, Diane stepped down from her platform. "I need to be on the same level, able to see and be seen by everyone."

This movement catalysed others. Both Alisha and Robert turned to face each other, though they maintained their distance. Emma stepped out from between them, standing alongside rather than between. Vincent moved from behind Diane to beside her. Michael took several steps closer to the group.

"Now what do you notice?" Elena asked as they settled into this new arrangement.

"I can breathe more easily," Alisha observed with surprise. "Just turning to face Robert directly has changed something."

"I feel less alone in my position," Robert added. "Even though we still disagree, there's something different about facing each other."

"There's more possibility in this configuration," Diane noted. "We're not aligned yet, but at least we can see each other fully."

Elena invited them to return to their seats, carrying this embodied experience with them. As they settled back into the circle, a subtle but distinct shift occurred in their presence – there were more direct eye contact, more relaxed postures and more authentic engagement.

"What just happened in that experiment," Elena explained, "is what Gestalt calls increasing awareness. You've made visible a pattern that was operating outside your awareness, and in doing so, created the possibility for choice where there was none before." She continued, "Now I'd like to focus on what seems most pressing in your field right now – what Gestalt would call the 'figure' that's emerging against the 'ground' of everything else happening at Somatech. What stands out as needing attention?"

"The breakdown in trust between Research and the Office of the CSO," Emma offered immediately.

Vincent nodded in agreement. "That's been the most visible issue around Neurocell."

"I wonder if that's the presenting issue, but not the core one," Michael suggested thoughtfully. "It feels like something about how scientific and commercial considerations are weighted in our decisions – not just with Neurocell but across our pipeline."

Elena turned to Robert and Alisha. "I'm noticing that when the tension between your departments was named, you both had visible reactions. Robert, you leaned back slightly. Alisha, you crossed your arms. I'm curious about what's happening for each of you right now."

"I feel defensive again," Robert admitted. "Ready to explain why my perspective on the Neurocell data was valid despite Alisha's objections."

"And I feel dismissed," Alisha acknowledged. "Like my team's four years of work on this molecule counts for less than a last-minute reinterpretation."

"Those are important awarenesses," Elena affirmed. "And I'm wondering if you'd be willing to try another experiment. Rather than debating the Neurocell data itself, would you be willing to take turns expressing what you needed from each other in that situation that you didn't receive?"

Both Robert and Alisha nodded, though with visible apprehension.

"Robert, would you be willing to start?" Elena asked. "Looking directly at Alisha, can you express what you needed from her around the Neurocell decision?"

Robert turned to face Alisha directly. After a moment's consideration, he spoke with unexpected openness. "I needed you to be willing to consider a different interpretation of the data without immediately dismissing it as scientifically unsound. I needed you to recognise that my perspective wasn't just about pushing the project forward at any cost, but about seeing potential that the standard analysis might miss."

Elena turned to Alisha. "Can you reflect back what you heard Robert saying?"

Alisha nodded. "You needed me to be more open to your interpretation and to trust that your motivation was scientific discovery, not just advancement at any cost." She paused. "And I didn't give you that."

"Now," Alisha prompted, looking directly at Robert, "can you express what you needed from him?"

Alisha met Robert's gaze. "I needed you to respect the rigorous analysis my team had already conducted before bringing an alternative interpretation directly to the board. I needed acknowledgment that our concerns weren't bureaucratic resistance but genuine scientific caution about under-powered data. I needed partnership rather than circumvention."

"Robert, can you reflect what you heard?" Elena asked.

"You needed respect for your team's work and process," Robert summarised. "You needed me to bring my concerns to you first, as a partner, rather than going around you to the board. And you felt I was dismissing your scientific judgment rather than supplementing it."

A palpable shift occurred as they spoke directly to each other rather than about each other. The rest of the team watched with rapt attention as the conflict that had been simmering beneath the surface was given direct expression.

"What's happening for each of you now?" Elena asked after a moment.

"I feel . . . seen," Robert said with mild surprise. "Even though we still disagree about Neurocell, there's something different in being heard about what I needed."

"I feel less angry," Alisha admitted. "And I can see that both of us were acting from commitment to scientific integrity, just with different approaches."

Elena turned to the rest of the team. "What are you noticing as you witness this exchange?"

"They're talking about needs and experience rather than positions," Diane observed. "And I realise how rarely we do that as a leadership team. We debate data and strategies, but not what we actually need from each other to function effectively."

"I notice I've been physically tensing and relaxing as they spoke," Vincent added. "Their interaction is affecting me bodily, not just intellectually."

"What you're experiencing," Elena explained, "is the difference between talking about a conflict and actually making contact around it. In Gestalt terms, contact occurs when we meet each other authentically at what we call the 'boundary' – the place where I end, and you begin."

She continued, "The Neurocell situation revealed not just a disagreement about data, but a boundary issue in how scientific and commercial perspectives meet in this organisation. Right now, that boundary seems rigid and polarised, with limited exchange between different viewpoints."

"That's exactly it," Michael affirmed. "It's as if we've created impermeable membranes between departments rather than semi-permeable ones that allow exchange while maintaining appropriate differentiation."

"So how do we make these boundaries more . . . permeable?" Diane asked.

"It begins with awareness," Elena replied. "You're already demonstrating that today – becoming aware of how you've been functioning and experimenting with alternatives. The next step is examining what Gestalt calls 'contact interruptions' – the ways we prevent ourselves from making genuine contact with each other."

She turned to the full circle. "For instance, I noticed earlier that when Robert and Alisha were expressing their needs, Emma physically leaned forward as if ready to intervene or mediate. That might be a pattern of 'introjection' – taking on responsibility that belongs to others."

Emma nodded with recognition. "That's exactly what I do. I try to smooth conflicts between others rather than letting them work it through themselves."

"And I notice I often deflect," Vincent acknowledged. "When tensions arise, I redirect to financial analyses rather than engaging with the emotional content of discussions."

"These patterns aren't wrong," Elena emphasised. "They're creative adjustments you've made to manage challenging situations. The question is whether they're still serving your collective purpose or limiting your contact and effectiveness."

As the session continued, Elena guided the team through additional experiments designed to increase awareness of their contact patterns. They explored how communication flowed or became blocked around the Neurocell decision, physically mapping the movement of information through the system and noticing where energy got stuck or diverted. Throughout, Elena kept the focus not on abstract analysis or future planning but on immediate experience – what was happening in the room, in their bodies, in their interactions moment by moment. When old patterns of intellectual debate or blame began to emerge, she gently redirected attention back to present awareness: "What are you experiencing right now as you say that?" or "What happens in your body when you hear that perspective?"

As they approached the end of their session, Elena invited a final reflection. "What's most figural for each of you now, as we prepare to close?"

"I'm aware of feeling more grounded," Alisha offered. "Like I'm standing on something solid even though many questions about Neurocell remain unresolved."

"I notice I'm breathing more fully," Robert added. "And making eye contact more easily, not just with Alisha but with everyone."

"I feel both relieved and challenged," Diane acknowledged. "There's clarity emerging about how we've been functioning that's uncomfortable but necessary."

"I'm aware of feeling more . . . present," Vincent said. "More emotionally engaged than I typically allow myself to be in leadership discussions."

"And I notice I'm in contact in a way I wasn't at the beginning," Michael concluded. "Not just observing from a distance."

Elena nodded, taking in these reflections. "What's emerged today isn't a strategic plan for Neurocell or a set of action items, but increased awareness of how you've been functioning and what might be possible with more conscious choice." She continued, "The polarisation between scientific and commercial perspectives isn't something to eliminate – both are essential to Somatech's purpose. The question is how to create more permeable boundaries between these perspectives so they can inform each other rather than opposing each other."

As the team members gathered themselves to leave, there was a tangible difference in how they moved and interacted. Diane paused to have a brief, direct conversation with Robert and Alisha together, not mediating but joining them in dialogue. Vincent engaged Michael in a conversation about regulatory perspectives, genuinely curious rather than distant. Emma moved with a more relaxed posture, not positioning herself as a buffer between potential conflicts. These subtle shifts reflected not a comprehensive transformation, but a meaningful step towards more authentic presence and contact – the beginning of a process rather than its completion. The Neurocell decision remained complex, but the team had discovered new possibilities for engaging with that complexity by bringing fuller awareness to how they worked together.

As Elena watched them depart, she reflected on the session. In Gestalt terms, what had occurred wasn't about solving problems or developing strategies, but about increasing awareness of what is – the first and most essential step towards meaningful change. The team hadn't "fixed" their conflict, but they had begun to see it clearly and to experience it directly rather than through the filters of projection and habitual response. And in that seeing, new possibilities had already begun to emerge.

Analysing the Session

This fictional team coaching session illustrates several core principles and techniques of Gestalt coaching applied in a team context. Let's analyse what transpired from the Gestalt perspective.

Present-Moment Awareness

The most fundamental Gestalt principle evident throughout the session is the emphasis on present-moment awareness – the "here and now":

Opening check-in: Elena begins by inviting team members to share "what you're experiencing right now, in this moment – physically, emotionally, mentally," immediately directing attention to immediate experience rather than analysis or planning.

Bodily awareness: She consistently guides team members to notice physical sensations – Diane's "tightness across my chest," Robert's tense jaw and Emma's held breath – helping them ground their awareness in embodied experience.

Tracking present experience: Throughout the session, Elena maintains focus on what's emerging in the moment rather than historical analysis. Questions like "What happens if you stay with that feeling of exposure?" keep team members in their present experience.

Here-and-now relationship: The tensions between team members are addressed as they manifest in the room, not just as historical issues. Elena notices and names real-time data, such as Robert leaning back and Alisha crossing her arms, when conflict is mentioned.

Paradoxical Change

The session demonstrates the Gestalt principle that change occurs through full awareness and acceptance of what is, not through trying to become something different.

Staying with what is: Rather than immediately trying to fix the team's problems, Elena encourages them to first become fully aware of their current patterns, inviting them to "notice this configuration" as they physically arrange themselves.

Awareness preceding action: The session prioritises awareness before planning. As Elena explains at the end, "What's emerged today isn't a strategic plan for

Neurocell or a set of action items, but increased awareness of how you've been functioning and what might be possible."

Change through awareness: Team members experience shifts not through deliberate techniques but through increased awareness, as when Alisha notes, "Just turning to face Robert directly has changed something."

Accepting polarities: Rather than trying to eliminate the tension between scientific and commercial perspectives, Elena helps the team see this as a natural polarity to be managed: "The polarisation between scientific and commercial perspectives isn't something to eliminate – both are essential to Somatech's purpose."

Experimental Approach

Gestalt coaching uses experiments to create embodied learning experiences, and several powerful experiments are evident in the session.

Circle arrangement: Beginning with a circle rather than the typical boardroom arrangement is itself an experiment that disrupts habitual patterns and makes new awareness possible.

Physical configuration: The experiment where team members arrange themselves to represent their functioning around Neurocell makes implicit patterns visible and tangible, creating immediate, embodied awareness.

One-move experiment: When Elena invites team members to "make one move – just one – to shift this configuration," she creates space for experimentation with new ways of being that emerge organically from awareness.

Needs expression: The experiment where Robert and Alisha directly express what they needed from each other creates a different quality of contact than their usual debate about data and positions.

Contact and Boundaries

Gestalt focuses on how people make contact with themselves, others and their environment, and boundary issues are central to the session:

Contact interruptions: Elena explicitly names patterns, such as Emma's "introjection" and Vincent's "deflection," as ways team members interrupt full contact with each other.

Boundary work: The session directly addresses what Elena calls "a boundary issue in how scientific and commercial perspectives meet in this organisation," helping members recognise both rigid boundaries ("impermeable membranes") and potential for more flexible ones ("semi-permeable ones that allow exchange").

Contact restoration: The work focuses on restoring healthy contact, evident when team members report feeling "more . . . present" and "in contact in a way I wasn't at the beginning."

Quality of contact: Elena attends to how contact occurs, noting that Robert and Alisha making "direct eye contact" and speaking "directly to each other rather than about each other" represents a significant shift in contact quality.

Figure-Ground Relationship

Gestalt coaching attends to what emerges as figural in the team's field of awareness.

Identifying the figure: Elena explicitly asks, "What is most pressing in your field right now – what Gestalt would call the 'figure' that's emerging against the 'ground' of everything else happening at Somatech."

Shifting figure: Throughout the session, there was a figural shift – from the initial awareness of physical presence, to the conflict between research and the CSO, to a deeper exploration of how scientific and commercial perspectives intersect with the organisation.

Closing with the present figure: The session ends by checking what's "most figural for each of you now," honouring that each person may have a different emergent awareness after the shared experience.

Background becoming figure: Issues that were previously in the background (like Emma's pattern of mediating or Vincent's emotional detachment) become figural through the coaching process, allowing them to be addressed directly.

Polarities and Integration

Gestalt recognises that human systems often organise around polarities, and this session reveals several important polarities within the team.

Scientific versus commercial: The central polarity is between scientific rigour (represented by Alisha) and commercial advancement (partially represented by Robert), which have become artificially opposed rather than integrated.

Safety versus risk: Underlying the Neurocell conflict is a polarity between caution (Alisha's concern about "under-powered data") and bold action (Robert seeing "potential where the standard analysis might miss it").

Individual versus collective: The tension between departmental perspectives and organisational needs represents a polarity that requires integration rather than resolution in favour of one pole or the other.

Distance versus engagement: Michael's positioning "at a distance from everyone" versus being fully engaged represents a polarity that many team members navigate in different ways.

The Coach's Gestalt Approach

In Gestalt, the coaching relationship itself serves as a model and catalyst for change. Several aspects of the coach's approach are particularly noteworthy.

- Modelling awareness: Elena demonstrates the quality of presence and awareness she's inviting from the team, modelling how to attend to present experience rather than getting caught in analysis or blame.
- Co-creating the process: Rather than imposing a rigid structure, Elena follows what emerges from the team, co-creating the coaching process based on what becomes figural in each moment.

- Working with resistance: When resistance emerges (like the initial silence after her invitation to share), Elena works with it as information rather than as an obstacle, gently inviting deeper engagement without forcing it.
- Using self as instrument: Elena uses her own awareness and experience as data about what's happening in the team system, noticing her own responses and using them as information about patterns that might otherwise remain invisible.

Key Shifts During the Session

Several pivotal moments represent significant shifts in the team's awareness and functioning.

Spatial reconfiguration: The initial circle arrangement disrupts habitual patterns and creates immediate awareness of typical communication patterns.

Embodied recognition: The physical configuration experiment creates a visceral recognition of team polarisation that intellectual discussion couldn't achieve.

From positions to needs: When Robert and Alisha express what they need from each other rather than debating data, they establish more authentic contact that shifts their relationship.

Boundary awareness: The recognition of "impermeable membranes between departments" versus "semi-permeable ones" represents a breakthrough in understanding how the team functions as a system.

Contact interruption identification: Team members recognising their habitual ways of interrupting contact (Emma's introjection, Vincent's deflection) creates the possibility for more conscious choices.

Outcomes and Emerging Directions

The session leads to several important outcomes consistent with Gestalt coaching:

Increased awareness: Team members develop greater awareness of their patterns, both individually and collectively. This awareness itself constitutes change from a Gestalt perspective.

More authentic presence: Each person becomes more fully present – physically, emotionally and intellectually – rather than compartmentalising or withholding aspects of their experience.

Improved contact: The quality of contact between team members visibly improves, with more direct communication, better eye contact and more authentic expression replacing defensive postures.

Self-regulation: Rather than being given strategies or techniques to implement, the team experiences how their natural self-regulation emerges through awareness, exemplified by the spontaneous shifts in physical positioning during the configuration experiment.

Integration of polarities: Previously polarised aspects of the team begin to integrate – scientific and commercial perspectives, individual and collective needs – creating the foundation for more holistic functioning.

Unlike other approaches that primarily focus on problem-solving or action-planning, the Gestalt coaching session addresses how team members are present with themselves, each other and the Neurocell challenge. It doesn't provide prescriptive solutions, but it helps the team develop more awareness, contact and presence. This creates conditions for organic change to emerge.

The session demonstrates how Gestalt coaching in a team context isn't about techniques or strategies but about helping the team become more fully aware of their current functioning so that natural movement towards health and effectiveness can occur. As Elena notes at the end, the team hasn't "fixed" their conflict in a traditional sense, but they have begun to see it clearly. In Gestalt terms, this awareness itself is the most essential precursor to meaningful change.

Chapter 13

Cognitive Team Coaching – *Patterns of Thought*

The executive conference room at Neurocell Pharmaceuticals' research headquarters hummed with subtle tension as the senior leadership team assembled. Through the floor-to-ceiling windows, morning light illuminated the polished walnut table where they gathered, their postures and expressions betraying varying degrees of discomfort and anticipation.

Dr. Naomi Reynolds, the cognitive coach who had been working with the company for three months, noticed the subtle cues as the executives arranged themselves around the oval table – who sat beside whom, who maintained physical distance and the quality of eye contact or its deliberate absence. She placed her notepad on the table and waited for the last team members to settle in.

"Thank you all for making time for our session today," Naomi began, her voice calm. "As we discussed last week, we're going to focus on your collective thinking processes around strategic decisions, particularly in light of the challenges that emerged during the Somatech project decision."

Diane Marshall, the CEO, nodded tersely. Her usual poised demeanour showed signs of strain – a tightness around her eyes, fingers drumming briefly on the tabletop before she consciously stilled them. "That seems necessary," she acknowledged. "The execution has been . . . problematic, shall we say."

"A diplomatic understatement," muttered Robert Chen, Chief Scientific Officer, just loudly enough to be heard. His expression betrayed frustration barely held in check.

Tension rippled visibly through the room. Dr. Alisha Patel, Head of Research, straightened in her chair, a flash of irritation crossing her face. "If by 'problematic' you mean that the subgroup analysis was submitted to the board without proper statistical validation, then yes, it was problematic."

"The data showed clear signals in that patient population," Robert countered, his voice rising slightly. "We can't ignore potential treatments because they don't fit our traditional statistical models."

"Enough," Diane interjected. "This is exactly what we need to address. We've been having the same circular arguments for weeks now."

Naomi nodded, taking in the exchange without judgement. "Rather than focusing immediately on the content of the disagreement, I'd like us to step back and

DOI: 10.4324/9781003594215-17

examine the thinking processes that might be operating here. What patterns do you notice in how you're approaching this situation as a team?"

The question was met with momentary silence. Michael Okafor, Head of Regulatory Affairs, broke it. "We're falling into position defence rather than problem-solving. Each department is defending its territory rather than looking at the scientific question as a whole."

"Interesting observation," Naomi responded. "I'm curious about the thinking that might be underneath that pattern. What assumptions might be driving that defensive stance?"

"Scientific integrity versus commercial opportunity," offered Vincent Torres, Chief Financial Officer, speaking for the first time. His analytical mind quickly identified the underlying dynamic. "Different departments believe their primary consideration should take precedence, so we're competing rather than collaborating. It's a clash of mental models."

"And why might those competing mental models be operating?" Naomi pressed, guiding them towards deeper metacognitive awareness.

A longer silence followed as the team considered this question. Diane finally responded, her voice more measured than before. "Because we haven't explicitly acknowledged that both scientific rigor and therapeutic potential are essential aspects of our mission. We've allowed them to be positioned as opposing values rather than complementary ones." She paused, a flash of insight crossing her face. "And as CEO, I haven't created enough space for integrating these perspectives before decisions reach crisis points."

"That's a powerful observation," Naomi noted. "You're recognising how leadership communication might be shaping the team's thinking framework. What other thinking patterns might be influencing how you approached the Somatech decision?"

Alisha leaned forward, her scientific mind engaging with the question. "We've been using an absolute threshold approach to data interpretation when perhaps a more nuanced framework might be appropriate for certain therapeutic areas. When unexpected signals emerged in the subgroup, we kept trying to apply our standard statistical models rather than developing a more specialised approach."

"Say more about the thinking behind that approach," Naomi encouraged.

"It's . . . almost a certainty bias," Alisha continued, the insight developing as she spoke. "We created detailed statistical parameters upfront and became anchored to them. Each deviation was treated as a potential error rather than as new information that might require a different analytical framework."

Robert nodded slowly, his earlier defensiveness fading as he engaged with this systems-level analysis. "And Research operates with a different mental model than Clinical Development. Research prioritises methodological purity, while Development is more willing to pursue signals that might benefit patients, even with higher uncertainty."

Naomi drew a simple diagram on her notepad and turned it so everyone could see. "You're identifying different thinking frameworks operating simultaneously in your team. This cognitive diversity can be a strength, but only if it's made explicit and leveraged intentionally. Instead, it appears these different mental models have been operating unconsciously, creating friction rather than synergy."

Emma Lawson, Head of Commercial Operations, studied the diagram. "So, Research's evidence-based thinking, Robert's possibility thinking, Regulatory's risk-management thinking, and Commercial's market-oriented thinking are all valid but potentially in conflict when not explicitly aligned."

"That's starting to get at the metacognitive awareness we're aiming for," Naomi confirmed. "You're beginning to notice not just what you think about Somatech, but how you think, both individually and collectively."

The team appeared energised by this shift in perspective, sitting up straighter and engaging more directly with each other. The focus on thinking processes rather than blame had visibly reduced defensive postures.

"I'd like to try a structured thinking exercise," Naomi suggested. "Let's map out the different cognitive approaches you each brought to the Somatech decision and see where there might have been misalignment."

Over the next 30 minutes, Naomi guided the team through an exercise, where each functional leader identified their primary criteria for decision-making, information-gathering processes and methods for evaluating evidence. These were captured visually on a shared digital whiteboard, creating a map of the team's cognitive diversity. As patterns emerged, so did realisations. Diane's expression showed growing awareness as she recognised how her own emphasis on definitive decisions had inadvertently created a climate where nuanced scientific discussion felt unwelcome. Alisha acknowledged how her methodological focus on statistical significance had made it difficult to integrate emerging signals that didn't meet predetermined thresholds. Robert saw how his emphasis on therapeutic possibility hadn't been effectively communicated in terms that would resonate with research's evidence-oriented framework.

"This is . . . illuminating," Diane said, studying the completed map. "We've been operating with fundamentally different thinking processes without ever making those explicit."

"And assuming bad intent when it was actually just different cognitive frameworks," added Alisha, with a brief apologetic glance towards Robert.

"What's becoming clear," Naomi observed, "is that your conflict isn't primarily about Somatech itself, but about unaligned thinking processes that led to different expectations, priorities, and approaches to evidence evaluation."

Vincent, who had been quietly analysing the patterns, spoke up. "There's another layer here too. Our thinking was siloed not just by functional area but also temporally. Research was focused on methodological validity for future decisions, Clinical was thinking about immediate patient impact, and Commercial was considering long-term market positioning. We were literally thinking in different timeframes."

"Excellent observation," Naomi smiled. "That temporal dimension of cognitive diversity is often overlooked but critically important. What might change if you explicitly aligned your thinking timeframes for pipeline decisions?"

"We could create much more realistic expectations," Robert suggested, the tension in his voice noticeably reduced. "If we acknowledged upfront that Research evaluates according to methodological standards while Clinical Development considers potential patient impact, we could build that reality into our evaluation process rather than treating it as a conflict."

"And we could leverage the strengths of different thinking styles instead of seeing them as obstacles," added Michael. "Research's methodological rigor, Clinical's patient focus, Regulatory's risk management, Commercial's market understanding – these are all valuable when integrated effectively."

Naomi nodded. "You're demonstrating cognitive flexibility now – the ability to shift thinking frames and see value in diverse approaches. That's one of the key states of mind we work to develop in cognitive coaching."

"This is helpful for understanding what happened," Diane acknowledged, "but how do we apply this going forward? We still have to make a decision about Somatech's development path."

"An excellent question that brings us to the practical application," Naomi responded. "Let's design a decision-making framework that intentionally incorporates your cognitive diversity rather than being undermined by it."

For the next portion of the session, Naomi guided the team in developing a more integrated approach to pipeline decisions. They created a structured process that began with explicit sharing of mental models and evaluation criteria, established a common understanding of how different types of evidence would be weighted, and built in regular recalibration points to incorporate emerging data within an adaptive framework. As they worked, the atmosphere in the room transformed. The defensive postures and tense exchanges of the beginning had given way to engaged collaboration. The focus on thinking processes rather than blame had created sufficient psychological safety for genuine problem-solving.

"I notice a significant shift in how you're working together now compared to when we started," Naomi observed. "What's changed in your collective thinking?"

"We're operating from a multi-frame perspective rather than a single-framework one," Alisha replied. "Looking at how our thinking patterns interact rather than just defending our individual mental models."

"And there's more inquiry, less advocacy," added Robert. "We're asking more questions about each other's thought processes instead of just pushing our own conclusions."

"Those are important shifts," Naomi says. "You're demonstrating greater metacognitive awareness – thinking about your thinking – which creates more possibilities for alignment even amid diversity."

As the session drew to a close, Diane addressed her team with renewed clarity. "I think we've uncovered something fundamental today. Our Somatech challenges weren't just scientific disagreements – they revealed misalignment in how we think and evaluate evidence as a leadership team. That's what we need to address if we want different results going forward." She turned to Naomi. "Can we develop a concrete protocol for our next major pipeline decision that incorporates what we've learned today? Something that explicitly aligns our thinking processes from the outset?"

"Absolutely," Naomi replied. "That would be a valuable application of today's insights. What if we use our next session to design that protocol together, building on the cognitive map we've created today?"

As the team members gathered their materials to leave, the shift in energy was palpable. They moved and spoke with greater ease; the earlier tension largely dissipated. Not because their scientific challenges had disappeared, but because they had gained a new cognitive framework for understanding and addressing them. Naomi noticed Alisha and Robert lingering after others had left, engaged in a conversation that appeared focused on integration rather than opposition. Emma and Vincent walked out together, discussing how to better align commercial timelines with research processes. Diane remained in her seat for a moment, reviewing the cognitive map with thoughtful attention.

"This is just the beginning," Naomi commented as Diane finally gathered her things. "Developing metacognitive skills is an ongoing process, not a one-time fix."

"I understand that now," Diane replied. "We've been trying to solve a thinking problem with more data, which explains our lack of progress." She smiled slightly. "It's ironic – as scientists and healthcare leaders, we pride ourselves on evidence-based decisions, yet we've never explicitly examined how we think about evidence together." As they walked towards the door, Diane added, "I've always approached team issues as either scientific disagreements or interpersonal conflicts. It never occurred to me they might be cognitive at their core."

"That's not unusual," Naomi assured her. "Our thinking processes are like water to fish – so pervasive we rarely notice them until someone helps us see them from a different perspective."

Diane nodded, a new determination evident in her posture. "Well, we've seen them now. And that changes everything about how we approach Somatech and future pipeline decisions."

Analysing the Session

This team coaching session illustrates several core principles and techniques of cognitive coaching applied in a team context. Let's analyse what transpired from a cognitive coaching perspective.

Focus on Thinking Processes

The most distinctive feature of this coaching session is its explicit focus on the team's thinking processes rather than on content, personalities or emotions:

Metacognitive emphasis: Naomi consistently directs attention to how team members think, not just what they think. Her opening frames the session as focusing on "your collective thinking processes around strategic decisions" rather than debating the merits of the Somatech project.

Mental models mapping: The visual mapping of each functional leader's "thinking frameworks" makes their implicit mental models explicit and visible for examination, a classic cognitive coaching technique.

Process over content: Throughout the session, Naomi maintains focus on cognitive processes rather than the scientific disagreement itself, emphasising that their conflict "isn't primarily about Somatech itself, but about unaligned thinking processes."

Thinking diversity recognition: The coach helps the team recognise that they weren't just having different opinions but operating with "fundamentally different thinking frameworks," highlighting the cognitive diversity within the team.

Cognitive Patterns and Distortions

The session identifies several cognitive patterns that influenced the team's approach to the Somatech decision.

Certainty bias: Alisha recognises how research became "anchored to" predetermined statistical parameters, treating deviations "as potential error rather than as new information."

Position defence: Michael observes how team members were "falling into position defence rather than problem-solving," prioritising defending territory over collaborative thinking.

Mental model clash: Vincent identifies the underlying dynamic as "a clash of mental models" between scientific integrity and commercial opportunity perspectives.

Temporal misalignment: Vincent's insight about how the team was "thinking in different timeframes" reveals an important cognitive dimension that had been completely invisible.

By identifying all these specific cognitive patterns, Naomi helps the team recognise systemic thinking tendencies rather than just addressing the isolated Somatech disagreement.

Cognitive coaching focuses on developing two key states of mind, both of which are addressed in this session: *Flexibility*: The team develops greater cognitive flexibility as they learn to recognise and appreciate different thinking styles. Robert demonstrates this when he acknowledges how integrating research's methodological rigour with Clinical Development's patient focus could be valuable. *Efficacy*: As the team develops an integrated decision framework, they build greater confidence in their ability to make complex decisions together. This growing sense of efficacy is apparent in their engagement with future applications.

Mediative Questioning Technique

Naomi also demonstrates skilled use of mediative questioning – questions designed to promote thinking rather than direct it. Such as:

- Open-ended cognitive questions: Her questions consistently focus on think-ing processes: "What patterns do you notice in how you're approaching this situation as a team?" and "What assumptions might be driving that defensive stance?"
- Building on responses: Her questions build on team members' responses, tak-ing their thinking deeper: When Vincent identifies competing mental models, Naomi asks, "And why might those competing mental models be operating?"
- Promoting connections: Her questions encourage team members to connect ideas and see patterns: "What might change if you explicitly aligned your think-ing timeframes for pipeline decisions?"

Cognitive coaching emphasises the use of specific, observable data rather than gen-eralisations or judgements. Throughout the session, Naomi helps the team identify specific thinking patterns – like certainty bias, position defence and temporal mis-alignment – providing concrete data about their cognitive processes. Finally, the mapping exercise creates a visual representation of the team's thinking processes, making abstract cognitive patterns into concrete, observable data that the team can analyse together.

Key Shifts in the Session

Several pivotal moments represent significant shifts in the team's thinking:

- From content to process: The initial shift from debating Somatech data to exam-ining thinking processes represents a fundamental cognitive change.
- Recognising implicit assumptions: Diane's realisation that she hadn't "created enough space for integrating these perspectives" shows growing awareness of how leadership assumptions shape team cognition.
- Identifying temporal misalignment: Vincent's observation that they were "think-ing in different timeframes" represents a sophisticated cognitive insight about a dimension of their thinking that had been completely invisible.
- From advocacy to enquiry: Robert notes that they are now asking "more questions about each other's thought processes instead of just pushing our own conclusions," marking a significant shift in their approach to communication.
- Metacognitive recognition: Diane's final insight that their challenges were "cog-nitive at their core" demonstrates a high-level metacognitive awareness that cre-ates possibilities for new approaches.

The Coach's Cognitive Approach

Naomi demonstrates several key aspects of cognitive coaching technique:

1. Trust in internal resources: Rather than offering solutions, Naomi consist-ently signals her belief that the team have the internal resources to solve their

own problems, needing only support to access their collective wisdom and intelligence.

2. Cognitive focus rather than emotional: While acknowledging tensions, Naomi keeps the primary focus on thinking processes rather than emotional processing or interpersonal dynamics.

3. Structured thinking tools: The cognitive mapping exercise provides concrete support for making thinking processes more explicit and examining them collectively.

4. Mediative rather than directive: Throughout the session, Naomi takes a mediative stance – facilitating the team's thinking rather than directing it towards predetermined conclusions.

Addressing Team Cognitive Dynamics

The session also reveals several team-specific cognitive patterns that Naomi helps the team recognise and address. For example, the team discovers they've been operating in cognitive silos – not just functional ones – with different mental models, temporal perspectives and evaluation criteria. They identify collective assumptions operating beneath the surface, such as the positioning of scientific rigour and therapeutic potential as opposing rather than complementary values. Rather than trying to eliminate cognitive differences, Naomi helps the team recognise how diverse thinking approaches can become a strength when made explicit and integrated intentionally. The team also identifies shared cognitive biases, such as the certainty bias Alisha describes where "each deviation was treated as a potential error rather than as new information."

Outcomes and Emerging Directions

By the end of the session, several important cognitive coaching outcomes are evident.

1. Enhanced metacognitive awareness: Team members demonstrate greater awareness of their own and others' thinking processes, creating the foundation for more effective collaboration.

2. Cognitive integration: The team begins developing frameworks that integrate their diverse thinking styles rather than allowing them to conflict unconsciously.

3. Increased cognitive flexibility: Members show greater ability to shift between different thinking perspectives, appreciating the value of diverse cognitive approaches.

4. Transfer of learning: The team begins planning how to apply their metacognitive insights to future pipeline decisions, indicating potential for transfer beyond the immediate Somatech situation.

5. Collective efficacy: The visible shift in energy and engagement by the end of the session reflects growing confidence in their ability to think and solve problems together effectively.

The session demonstrates the essence of cognitive coaching: developing awareness of thinking processes to enhance decision-making and problem-solving. Naomi doesn't tell the team what to think about Somatech but helps them recognise and refine how they think together.

What makes this distinctly cognitive coaching is the explicit focus on thinking processes themselves. Rather than focusing primarily on emotions, relationships or functional disagreements, Naomi consistently directs attention to cognitive patterns, mental models and metacognitive awareness. This focus ultimately empowers the team to approach their Somatech challenges with greater cognitive flexibility, efficacy and skill, creating sustainable improvement in their decision-making and collective team intelligence.

Part 4

Integrative Coaching

Chapter 14

Integrative Coaching

Integrative coaching is a holistic approach to leadership development that synthesises multiple coaching methodologies, psychological frameworks and developmental theories to address the full spectrum of a leader's professional and personal growth. Unlike approaches that adhere strictly to a single theoretical model, integrative coaching draws from diverse perspectives to create customised coaching tailored to each coachee's unique context, challenges and aspirations.

The integrative approach is built on the premise that effective personal and leadership development requires attention to multiple dimensions of human experience and organisational life. Rather than focusing exclusively on behaviour, cognition, emotions or systems, integrative coaches recognise that all these elements are interconnected and must be addressed as part of a coherent coaching approach.

The integrative philosophy embraces both the pragmatic focus on measurable results typical of business coaching and the deeper developmental focus that addresses the leaders' "inner theatre," that is, their mindset, emotions, identity and purpose. It is based on the assumption that sustainable leader effectiveness emerges from an alignment between external action and internal reality.

Dimensions of Integration

Integrative coaching typically bridges multiple theoretical frameworks, perspectives and techniques, which might include:

- Cognitive behavioural approaches for addressing thinking patterns and behaviours
- Psychodynamic perspectives for exploring unconscious patterns and motivations
- Systems thinking for understanding organisational dynamics and contexts
- Existential frameworks for engaging with questions of meaning and purpose
- Developmental models for recognising stages of leadership maturity
- Somatic approaches for accessing embodied wisdom and presence

DOI: 10.4324/9781003594215-19

Rather than rigidly applying a single methodology, the integrative coach moves fluidly between perspectives based on what will best serve the client's development at any given moment.

Integrative coaching addresses both the "doing" aspects of leadership (skills, behaviours, results etc.) and the "being" dimensions (presence, mindset, identity and values). It recognises that sustainable leadership effectiveness emerges from the alignment of these dimensions rather than from focusing on either in isolation. For example, an integrative coach might help an executive develop specific communication skills (doing) while also exploring how their sense of identity or purpose influences their communication style (being). The approach connects an executive's inner experience (thoughts, emotions, values and purpose) with their outer reality (actions, relationships, systems and results), recognising that effective leadership requires coherence between all of these realms.

Rather than maintaining artificial boundaries between "professional coaching" and "personal coaching," integrative coaching recognises that leadership effectiveness is influenced by the whole person. An integrative coach might help a leader recognise how their internal assumptions shape their perception of external challenges or how organisational systems influence their internal states and behaviours. While maintaining appropriate focus on professional goals, it acknowledges that personal dimensions – including health, relationships and life purpose – significantly impact leadership capacity. The integrative approach balances immediate performance goals with longer-term developmental trajectories. It helps leaders address current challenges while simultaneously building capacities that will serve them across their whole professional journey.

Benefits of the Integrative Approach

- Integrative coaching offers several advantages compared to more narrowly focused approaches, such as:
- Customisation to Individual Needs – by drawing from multiple methodologies, the integrative approach can be precisely tailored to each leader's unique developmental needs, learning style and personal preferences.
- Addressing Root Causes, Not Just Symptoms – the multidimensional perspective helps identify underlying patterns that may be causing surface-level challenges. Rather than simply addressing symptoms, integrative coaching can work at the level of root causes.
- Adaptability to Changing Circumstances – as the leader faces new challenges or experiences, the integrative coach can flexibly adapt the approach to address emerging needs rather than being constrained by a single methodology.
- Sustainable Development – by addressing multiple dimensions simultaneously, integrative coaching can produce more sustainable results than approaches that focus on behaviour change alone without addressing underlying mindset or systemic factors.

- Whole-Person Development – the integrative approach honours the complexity of human experience, helping individuals develop not just as functional leaders but also as whole persons bringing their full capacities to their leadership roles.

Coach Capabilities

Effective integrative coaching can be demanding and requires a coach to possess a breadth and depth of skill and knowledge. For example:

- Theoretical insight: Deep knowledge of multiple coaching methodologies and psychological frameworks
- Contextual understanding: Appreciation of organisational dynamics, business realities and leadership challenges
- Developmental perspective: Recognition of how personal and leadership capacities evolve over time
- Systemic awareness: Ability to see patterns in complex human and organisational systems
- Presence and adaptability: Capacity to work fluidly with whatever emerges in the coaching relationship

These kinds of capabilities are required, as in practice, an integrative coach might, for example, work with a leader who is struggling with strategic decision-making by:

- Exploring the cognitive frameworks shaping how they process information (cognitive approach)
- Examining how organisational dynamics influence their decision process (systems perspective)
- Addressing emotional reactions that might be clouding judgement (emotional intelligence focus)
- Connecting decisions to deeper purpose and values (existential dimension)

Rather than seeing these as separate interventions, the integrative coach can weave them together into a coherent developmental experience that recognises the interconnected nature of all these dimensions.

In summary, integrative coaching represents a sophisticated approach to leadership development that transcends the limitations of single-methodology coaching. By drawing from multiple perspectives and addressing the multidimensional nature of leadership, it offers executives and others a comprehensive path to enhanced effectiveness and fulfilment. While demanding greater breadth and flexibility from the coach, this approach is particularly well-suited to the complex challenges facing today's leaders, who must navigate rapidly changing environments that demand the full spectrum of human potential.

Synthesising Cognitive, Gestalt, Existential and Systems-Psychodynamic Approaches

An integrative executive coach who specifically synthesises cognitive, gestalt, existential and systems-psychodynamic approaches creates a particularly powerful coaching methodology that addresses the thinking patterns, present-moment awareness, meaning dimensions and unconscious systemic dynamics of leadership. This specific integration enables a comprehensive approach to executive development that acknowledges both the individual leader's internal experience and their embeddedness in wider organisational systems.

The effective integration of these four (and other) approaches is based on recognising their complementary strengths. As a reminder:

- Cognitive coaching excels at identifying and refining thinking patterns that influence decision-making and leadership effectiveness.
- Gestalt coaching brings powerful present-moment awareness and experiential learning that reveals patterns outside conscious awareness.
- Existential coaching addresses deeper questions of meaning, purpose, authenticity and choice that underpin leadership actions.
- Systems-psychodynamic coaching reveals unconscious organisational dynamics and how leaders both shape and are shaped by these systemic forces.

Rather than compartmentalising these approaches, the integrative coach weaves them together, recognising that leadership challenges typically involve them all simultaneously; thinking patterns, immediate experience, questions of meaning and systemic dynamics.

The skilled integrative executive coach can leverage the specific complementary elements of these approaches: that is,

- Cognitive and Gestalt Integration
    When cognitive coaching's focus on thinking patterns is combined with Gestalt's emphasis on present-moment awareness, executives can both identify limiting thought patterns and experience their immediate impact. Cognitive coaching helps name thinking distortions like black-and-white thinking or catastrophising *and then* Gestalt approaches can bring awareness to how these thinking patterns manifest in the body and immediate experience. Together, they create both conceptual understanding and experiential recognition that accelerates change. For example, a leader struggling with impostor syndrome benefits from cognitively identifying this thinking pattern while also becoming aware of how it manifests in real time during important meetings – tension in the shoulders, held breath and diminished presence etc.
- Existential and Cognitive Integration
    The combination of existential coaching's focus on meaning and choice with cognitive coaching's emphasis on thinking patterns helps executives align their

leadership with deeper values while recognising limiting thought patterns. Existential coaching addresses fundamental questions of meaning, purpose and authentic choice, *and then* cognitive coaching identifies thinking patterns that prevent alignment with these deeper values. Together, they help executives make conscious choices aligned with purpose while managing sabotaging thoughts. For a leader contemplating a major career transition, this integration helps them clarify what truly matters (existential) while identifying and managing catastrophic thinking patterns that might prevent authentic choice (cognitive).

- Systems-Psychodynamic and Gestalt Integration

  The combination of systems-psychodynamic attention to organisational dynamics with Gestalt's present-moment awareness reveals how systemic patterns manifest in immediate experience. Systems-psychodynamic coaching identifies unconscious organisational dynamics and role-related pressures, *and then* Gestalt approaches bring awareness to how these dynamics manifest in present-moment experience. Together, they help executives recognise systemic patterns as they emerge in real time. A CEO experiencing tension with their board could benefit from understanding the unconscious systemic dynamics at play (systems-psychodynamic) while also becoming aware of their immediate defensive responses during board interactions (Gestalt).

- Existential and Systems-Psychodynamic Integration

  When existential coaching's focus on authentic choice meets systems-psychodynamic attention to organisational dynamics, executives can make meaningful choices while understanding systemic constraints. Existential coaching emphasises freedom and responsibility in leadership choices *and then* Systems-psychodynamic coaching reveals unconscious forces that influence these choices. Together, they help leaders exercise authentic choice within complex organisational realities. This integration helps a leader navigating organisational politics maintain authentic purpose (existential) while understanding the unconscious dynamics and social defences operating in their system (systems-psychodynamic).

Integrated Interventions in Practice

Below are some examples of a selection of exercises and interventions the integrative executive coach might employ:

Cognitive-Gestalt Experiments

These interventions combine cognitive awareness of thinking patterns with experiential Gestalt experiments; that is,

- Identifying a limiting belief through cognitive enquiry, then creating a Gestalt experiment to explore how this belief manifests physically and emotionally in the present moment

- Using physical movement or spatial arrangements to represent different thinking patterns, making abstract cognitive processes tangible and experiential
- Bringing immediate awareness to automatic thoughts as they arise during coaching interactions

For example, a leader who mentally dismisses positive feedback might identify this cognitive pattern and then experiment with physically standing in different positions representing "receiving" versus "dismissing" to develop embodied awareness of this pattern.

Existential-Cognitive Reflection

These interventions integrate meaning-focused existential enquiry with cognitive pattern recognition, that is,

- Exploring core values and purpose, then identifying cognitive distortions that prevent authentic expression of these values
- Examining how "should" statements and absolutist thinking limit freedom of authentic choice
- Developing cognitive flexibility in service of existential authenticity

A leader struggling with work-life balance might clarify what truly matters (existential) while identifying all-or-nothing thinking patterns that maintain an unsustainable approach to work (cognitive).

Systems-Gestalt Mapping

These interventions integrate systems-psychodynamic awareness with Gestalt experiential learning; that is,

- Creating physical representations of organisational dynamics that make unconscious patterns visible and tangible
- Using empty chair work to explore different roles and projections in the system
- Bringing present-moment awareness to how systemic pressures manifest in the body and immediate experience

For instance, as in the earlier case study, a leadership team might physically arrange themselves to represent current organisational dynamics, making unconscious patterns visible and creating immediate awareness of systemic tensions.

Existential-Systems Exploration

These interventions combine existential questions of meaning and choice with systems-psychodynamic understanding; that is,

- Exploring how organisational purpose aligns with personal meaning
- Examining how systemic roles influence authentic choice
- Identifying where freedom exists within systemic constraints

A leader considering organisational transformation might explore both the authentic purpose driving this change (existential) and the unconscious systemic forces that might support or undermine it (systems-psychodynamic).

The Integrated Coaching Relationship

As in all coaching, in this integrated approach, the coaching relationship itself becomes a powerful vehicle for development and change. But as with everything else in integrated coaching, the relationship must be attended to at various levels. For example, consider the following four lenses that could be considered when analysing the coach-coachee interaction:

- Cognitive awareness of patterns emerging in the coaching relationship
- Gestalt presence to the immediate experience of the coach and coachee together
- Existential authenticity in the coaching dialogue
- Systems-psychodynamic attention to how the coaching relationship might mirror organisational dynamics

If the coach has the integrative capacity to weave all of these approaches together coherently (rather than applying them in isolation) and has the contextual sensitivity to select real-time appropriate methodologies based on the executive's needs and readiness, then the coach can model integration by moving fluidly between these perspectives. While, at all times maintaining a coherent approach responsive to the coachee's emerging needs.

Conclusion

The integration of cognitive, Gestalt, existential and systems-psychodynamic approaches creates a particularly powerful approach to coaching that addresses the full spectrum of leadership development. By working simultaneously with thinking patterns, present experience, meaningful purpose and systemic dynamics, this integration supports coachees in developing greater effectiveness, authenticity and wisdom in navigating today's demanding leadership challenges.

This specific integrative approach is particularly valuable for senior executives facing complex challenges that cannot be adequately addressed through any single perspective. It honours both the individual leader's internal experience and their embeddedness in wider systems, creating development that is personally meaningful and organisationally impactful simultaneously.

Case Study: *Leader at the Crossroads*

Sarah Bennett embodied the rare blend of strategic acumen and prin-cipled commitment that had propelled her to the CEO position at Meridian Healthcare Systems. Known for her commanding presence and decisive leadership style, Sarah has spent 20 years climbing through the ranks of healthcare administration to reach this pinnacle of influence. Her professional journey has been driven by a powerful conviction that healthcare systems can serve communities profitably without sacrificing quality of care. This vision sets her apart from many industry peers.

Under her leadership, Meridian had developed a reputation for both operational excellence and ethical stewardship. While many of their healthcare competitors had pursued aggressive consolidation strate-gies that prioritised financial metrics over community service, Sarah attempted to chart a different course. Her leadership philosophy has emphasised sustainable growth balanced with community commitment, positioning Meridian as an industry outlier that investors respected and community stakeholders trusted.

This distinctive approach to healthcare leadership stems from Sarah's personal and professional background. She has had to work "against" hospital closures and service consolidations throughout her career and has witnessed more than her fair share of the negative impacts of purely profit-driven private healthcare earlier in her professional life. She had served in private health facilities that were acquired and sub-sequently downsized and had also worked in public health, where she observed the consequences of reduced healthcare funding in vulnerable communities.

Sarah's rise to CEO represents the culmination of carefully calculated career moves that required significant personal sacrifice. She had to navigate the complex, male-dominated healthcare leadership landscape with exceptional skill, overcoming obstacles and proving her value at each step. Her achievement of this leadership position wasn't merely for personal ambition but was fuelled by the belief that she could "make a difference at scale" – implementing her vision of balanced healthcare leadership from a position of real influence.

Now, six months into her CEO tenure, Sarah faces a defining chal-lenge that places her at a profound professional and personal cross-roads. The board's push for the Northstar acquisition, which would deliver the market growth and financial results shareholders expect, but require closing three rural hospitals and consolidating services, directly conflicts with the values that have guided her career. This situation creates not just a strategic dilemma but also an existential crisis about her identity as a leader and the authentic purpose of her work.

The Northstar decision represents far more than a typical business challenge; it serves as a crucible moment that will define not only the future direction of Meridian Healthcare but also Sarah's understanding of herself as a leader and the legacy she will ultimately leave in an industry where principled leadership is both desperately needed and exceedingly difficult to sustain.

An Integrative Coaching Session

As Sarah Bennett enters her coaching session with Dr. Maya Kazan, she carries the physical manifestations of this tension – hunched shoulders, shallow breathing and a disconnected gaze. The woman who typically projects confidence and clarity now finds herself constricted by competing imperatives and questioning whether her vision of balanced healthcare leadership is truly achievable or merely idealistic rhetoric that cannot withstand market pressures.

The 42nd floor office offered a panoramic view of the city, the afternoon light catching the glass façades of neighbouring office blocks. Inside, the carefully curated space – minimalist furniture, abstract art, a single bonsai tree on a side table – spoke of refined taste and controlled precision. Yet the atmosphere between the two people seated in ergonomic chairs by the floor-to-ceiling windows vibrated with an undercurrent of tension.

Sarah sat across from Dr. Kazan, the integrative executive coach she had been working with for six months. Maya observed both Sarah's posture and the quality of silence that had descended after Sarah described the board meeting that had left her questioning her leadership path.

"The board wants aggressive growth through the Northstar acquisition," Sarah had explained, her voice controlled but tight. "It makes financial sense on paper. The market expects it. But it would mean closing three rural hospitals and consolidating services. Hundreds of jobs lost. Communities with reduced access to care. Everything I've worked against my entire career." She'd fallen silent then, her gaze fixed on the cityscape below.

Maya let the silence breathe for a moment, noticing her own response to Sarah's dilemma – a tightening in her chest, a subtle holding of breath. Integrating both cognitive awareness and Gestalt presence, she began their session. "I notice as you describe this situation, your shoulders have drawn inward, your breathing has become shallow, and you're looking out at the city rather than making eye contact,"

Maya observed, bringing Gestalt awareness to the present moment. "I'm curious about what you're experiencing right now, in your body, as you hold this dilemma."

Sarah's gaze remained fixed on the horizon. "Constriction. Like I'm in a vice that's tightening from both sides." She placed a hand to her sternum. "A heaviness here. And a knot in my stomach."

"Stay with those sensations for a moment," Maya says. "The constriction, the heaviness, the knot. What happens if you simply allow them to be there, neither pushing them away nor trying to fix them?"

Sarah closed her eyes briefly, her attention turning inward. After several breaths, she spoke again, her voice softer. "The constriction is . . . pulsing. Not static. Behind it, there's anger. And beneath that, something that feels like grief."

"That's powerful awareness," Maya acknowledged. "You're recognising not just your thoughts about this situation but how you're carrying it in your body. What thoughts are accompanying these physical sensations?" With this question, Maya shifted towards a more cognitive approach, exploring the thinking patterns underlying Sarah's experience of constriction.

"That I've failed," Sarah admits, facing Maya directly for the first time since describing the board meeting. "That all my talk about ethical leadership and community commitment was just talk when real money is on the table. That I should have seen this coming and prepared better arguments. That I'm not cut out for this level of leadership if I can't align my values with business realities."

Maya smiled. "Those are significant thoughts. I'm hearing what sound like several cognitive patterns – black-and-white thinking in framing this as complete failure, 'should' statements about what you could have done differently, and some mind-reading about what this means about you as a leader. Would you be willing to examine these thoughts more closely?"

Sarah nodded, some of the tension in her face easing slightly at the prospect of concrete analysis.

"Let's start with the thought that you've failed. Is that objectively true? Has a final decision been made about the acquisition?"

"No," Sarah acknowledged. "The board expects my recommendation next month. They're strongly signalling their preference, but no, the decision hasn't been made."

"So, you're experiencing the thought 'I've failed' in a situation that's still unfolding," Maya observed. "What other perspectives might be possible here?"

Sarah considers this. "That I'm in the middle of a difficult challenge, not at the end of one. That tension between values and financial pressures is inherent in private healthcare leadership, not a sign of personal failure."

"Those alternative thoughts seem to create more space for possibility," Maya noted. "What shifts in your body as you consider them?"

"The vice loosens somewhat," Sarah said with mild surprise. "I can breathe a bit more fully."

Maya allowed this awareness to settle and then shifted towards a more existential perspective. "This situation seems to be bringing you face-to-face with some fundamental questions about meaning and choice in your leadership. What does this moment represent for you on your leadership journey?"

Sarah's expression grew contemplative. "It feels like a crossroads. A moment that will define not just the future of Meridian, but who I am as a leader." She paused and then added with unexpected intensity, "I took this role because I believed I could build a healthcare system that served communities profitably without sacrificing care. If I can't find that balance in this situation, what am I doing here?"

"That's a profound existential question," Maya says. "You're confronting not just a business decision but a question about your purpose and authentic expression as a leader."

Sarah's eyes narrow. "I've spent twenty years climbing to this position, believing I could make a difference at scale. Now I'm here, with real power, facing a classic dilemma – profit versus purpose – and I'm not sure I can resolve it any better than my predecessors."

Maya leaned forward slightly. "I hear the weight of that uncertainty. And I'm curious – is it possible that framing this as profit versus purpose is itself a limitation? What possibilities might emerge if we examined that either/or thinking?"

Sarah considered this, her strategic mind engaging with the cognitive reframe. "You're suggesting a false dichotomy. That perhaps there are approaches that serve both purpose and profit, not one at the expense of the other."

"I'm not suggesting any particular answer," Maya clarified, "but rather inviting exploration of whether the way you're framing the dilemma might be constraining possible solutions."

Sarah nodded slowly, then stood and moved to the window, her need for movement reflecting the energy shifting within her. "The board is thinking in quarterly terms. I've been thinking in annual terms. But building a truly sustainable healthcare system requires thinking in decades." Her voice grew stronger. "There are approaches to the Northstar integration that might preserve more services and jobs if we extended the timeline for ROI realisation."

Maya observed this shift, noting how cognitive reframing had created space for new strategic thinking. Now she moved to integrate a systems-psychodynamic perspective. "I'd like to explore another dimension of this situation," she suggested. "Healthcare systems, like all organisations, develop unconscious patterns for managing anxiety. I'm wondering what anxieties might be driving the board's push for aggressive consolidation, and what role you might be taking up in that unconscious system."

Sarah turned from the window, intrigued by this perspective. "What do you mean by unconscious patterns?"

"Organisations often displace anxiety about uncertainty onto specific decisions or individuals," Maya explained. "The healthcare industry faces enormous uncertainty right now – regulatory changes, technological disruption, staffing challenges. The board's fixation on this particular acquisition might be a way of creating an illusion of control amid that uncertainty."

Sarah's eyes widened with recognition. "And as CEO, I'm expected to either provide certainty by executing their preferred strategy or become the container for all the industry anxiety they're trying to escape."

"That's another powerful insight," Maya says. "You may be carrying something for the entire system – both the organisation's anxiety about financial viability and the communities' anxiety about access to care. Rather than just seeing this as your personal dilemma, what if it's a systemic pattern you're making visible through your leadership position?"

Sarah returned to her seat, her posture now more open, her movements more fluid. "So perhaps my discomfort is actually valuable data about the system, not just a personal failure to reconcile competing demands."

"Exactly," Maya said. "From a systems perspective, your experience might be revealing tensions that exist throughout healthcare but often remain unacknowledged." Maya noticed that this systems-psychodynamic perspective had created a different quality of energy in Sarah – less self-recrimination, more curious engagement. She decided to integrate a Gestalt experiment to deepen this emerging awareness. "I'd like to try something, if you're willing," Maya suggested. "Imagine that this room contains three positions: one representing the board's financial imperative, one representing community healthcare needs, and one representing your authentic leadership. Where would you place each position in this space, and where are you currently standing in relation to them?"

After considering the invitation, Sarah stood and began arranging the spaces. She pointed to the window overlooking the financial district. "The board's position is there, focusing outward on market expectations and industry trends." She moved to the opposite side of the room, near the door. "The community needs are here, at ground level, where people enter our facilities seeking care." Finally, she indicated a spot by her desk. "My authentic leadership would stand there – connected to both, but with a distinct perspective."

"And where are you actually standing right now?" Maya asked.

Sarah considered, then moved to a spot closer to the window. "Here. I've been pulled toward the board's perspective, feeling I need to align with them to maintain my credibility and influence."

"What happens if you physically move to the position you identified as your authentic leadership?" Maya invited.

Sarah walked deliberately to the spot by her desk. As she stood there, her posture shifted subtly – shoulders relaxing, spine straightening, feet planting more firmly on the ground.

"What do you notice now?" Maya asked.

"I can see both other positions from here," Sarah observed with surprise. "When I was standing near the board position, the community needs seemed distant, abstract. From here, I can hold both in my field of vision." She took a deep breath. "And I feel . . . centred. Less reactive. Like I'm standing on my own ground rather than being pulled toward either pole."

"That sounds significant," Maya says. "You're experiencing physically what it means to maintain your authentic position while staying in relationship with these competing demands. Not collapsed into either but holding your own space that can be in connection with both."

Sarah remained in the spot, her expression reflecting the internal shift that had occurred. "From here, I can see more possibilities. The board's financial concerns aren't wrong – we do need sustainable growth. And the community needs are real – not just idealistic abstractions. My job isn't to choose between them but to create a third way that honours both."

Maya observed this integration with a nod. "You're moving from an either/or mindset to a both/and perspective. How does that shift feel in your body compared to the constriction you described earlier?"

"Expansive," Sarah said, touching her sternum where the heaviness had been. "There's energy here now, not weight. And clarity, not confusion."

As Sarah returned to her seat, Maya drew their threads together, integrating the cognitive, Gestalt, existential and systems-psychodynamic dimensions of their exploration.

"In our session today, you've recognised thinking patterns that created a sense of failure and limitation. You've experienced physically what it means to stand in your authentic leadership rather than being pulled toward competing positions. You've connected with your fundamental purpose as a healthcare leader. And you've recognised how you might be carrying systemic tensions that extend beyond your individual leadership."

Sarah nodded, her presence now qualitatively different from the constricted CEO who had begun the session. "I still don't have all the answers for the Northstar situation, but I'm approaching it from a completely different place now."

"What's your next step from this new place?" Maya asked.

Sarah considered thoughtfully. "I need to meet individually with board members to understand the anxieties beneath their push for rapid consolidation. I need to develop alternative approaches that address financial imperatives while preserving more community services – perhaps through extended timelines or phased integration. And I need to remember to physically stand in my authentic leadership position when I present these alternatives, not collapse into either the board's position or an oppositional stance."

"Those sound like thoughtful next steps emerging from our different perspectives today," Maya affirmed. "And I'm curious, what are you taking away from this exploration on a more personal level?"

Sarah's expression softened. "A reminder that my leadership isn't just about what I do but how I stand in relationship to competing forces. When I feel that constriction again – and I will – it's a signal to check where I'm standing, what I'm thinking, and what might be happening in the larger system." She smiled slightly. "And perhaps most importantly, that crossroads moments like these aren't failures of leadership but the very essence of it."

As their session drew to a close, Maya noted how the integration of cognitive awareness, Gestalt experimentation, existential purpose and systems understanding had created a multidimensional shift for Sarah. The CEO gathering herself was noticeably different from the one who had entered – not because her external challenges had disappeared, but because her relationship to those challenges had fundamentally transformed.

Sarah paused at the door. "You know, I've been thinking about this Northstar situation as a tangled knot I needed to solve. Now I'm seeing it more as a tapestry I'm helping to weave – complex, requiring careful attention to many threads, but ultimately creating something of lasting value if I approach it with both care and courage."

Maya smiled at the metaphor, recognising in it the integration Sarah had achieved – holding complexity with clarity, purpose with pragmatism and authenticity with effectiveness – the essence of truly integrated leadership.

Analysing the Coaching Session

The coaching session between Dr. Maya Kazan and Sarah Bennett exemplifies a sophisticated integration of cognitive, Gestalt, existential and systems-psychodynamic approaches. The coaches' shifts between each of these were explicitly indicated to help the reader follow what was happening, but now let's go into more detail about what the coach chose to do and why. Let's analyse how these different methodologies were all woven together to create a transformative coaching experience for the executive.

The Presenting Challenge

Sarah entered the session struggling with a profound leadership dilemma: the board's pressure to pursue the Northstar acquisition, which made financial sense but contradicted her values by requiring service consolidation and the closure of several hospitals. This challenge created significant emotional and cognitive tension, manifesting as physical constriction and conflicting thoughts about her role and leadership effectiveness.

The coach began with a Gestalt here-and-now approach, focusing on Sarah's immediate, embodied experience. Maya observed and named Sarah's physical presentation: "[Y]our shoulders have drawn inward, your breathing has become shallow, and you're looking out at the city rather than making eye contact." She invited awareness of bodily sensations: "[W]hat you're experiencing right now, in your body, as you hold this dilemma." She encouraged staying with uncomfortable sensations: "What happens if you simply allow them to be there, neither pushing them away nor trying to fix them?" This Gestalt beginning established immediate presence and created a foundation of embodied awareness that revealed the physical manifestation of Sarah's dilemma as "constriction . . . heaviness . . . a knot in my stomach." By starting with present-moment, bodily experience, Maya bypassed intellectual defences and accessed deeper layers of Sarah's experience.

Building on this embodied awareness, Maya then shifted to a cognitive approach to explore Sarah's thinking patterns. She asked about thoughts accompanying physical sensations: "What thoughts are accompanying these physical sensations?" She identified specific cognitive distortions: "black-and-white thinking . . . 'should' statements . . . mind-reading" and used Socratic questioning to examine these thoughts: "Is that objectively true? Has a final decision been made about the acquisition?" She then facilitated the development of alternative perspectives: "What other perspectives might be possible here?" This cognitive work helped Sarah recognise how her thinking was creating a premature sense of failure and limiting her view of possibilities. The identification of the false dichotomy between profit and purpose was particularly significant, creating cognitive space for more nuanced approaches.

Once Sarah had greater awareness of both physical experience and thinking patterns, Maya integrated an existential dimension. She framed the situation in terms of meaning and choice: "This situation seems to be bringing you face-to-face with some fundamental questions about meaning and choice in your leadership." She explored the significance of this moment in Sarah's leadership journey: "What does this moment represent for you on your leadership journey?" and acknowledged the profound question of purpose: "You're confronting not just a business decision but a question about your purpose and authentic expression as a leader." This existential exploration connected Sarah's immediate challenge to her broader leadership purpose and authentic self-expression. Her recognition of this as a "crossroads" moment elevated the situation from a mere business decision to a defining expression of her leadership identity and values.

Building on the personal dimensions, Maya then expanded the focus by bringing in a systems-psychodynamic perspective. She introduced the concept of organisational anxiety: "Healthcare systems, like all organisations, develop unconscious patterns for managing anxiety." She explored systemic dynamics beyond individual psychology: "[W]hat anxieties might be driving the board's push for aggressive consolidation, and what role you might be taking up in that unconscious system?" She then reframed Sarah's personal struggle as potentially systemic: "[Y]ou may be carrying something for the entire system." This systems perspective significantly shifted Sarah's relationship to her challenge, helping her see her discomfort not as personal failure but as "valuable data about the system." This reduced self-recrimination and enabled more objective engagement with the underlying organisational dynamics.

To integrate these multidimensional insights, Maya returned to a Gestalt approach with an experiential exercise. She created a spatial representation of competing forces: "Imagine that this room contains three positions. . . ." She facilitated physical movement between positions: "What happens if you physically move to the position, you identified as your authentic leadership?" She then connected physical experience to leadership stance: "You're experiencing physically what it means to maintain your authentic position while staying in relationship with these competing demands." This embodied experiment consolidated the cognitive, existential and systemic insights into a tangible experience of standing in authentic leadership while maintaining a relationship with competing demands. Sarah's physical experience of feeling "centred" and being able to "see both other positions" made concrete her shift from either/or to both/and thinking.

Several moments in the session demonstrated the particularly powerful integration of multiple approaches.

Integration of Cognitive and Gestalt

Maya repeatedly connected thinking patterns to bodily experience – "What shifts in your body as you consider [these alternative thoughts]?" Sarah's recognition that "[t]he vice loosens somewhat. I can breathe a bit more fully," as her thinking shifted. This integration helped Sarah experience how cognitive shifts create immediate physical changes, making abstract thinking patterns tangible and accessible.

Integration of Existential and Systems-Psychodynamic

The session connected Sarah's personal purpose with systemic dynamics. Her existential question about making "a difference at scale" was linked to the system's unconscious patterns. Her authentic leadership position physically stood in relationship to both board concerns and community needs. This integration helped Sarah see how her personal leadership purpose could be expressed within complex systemic dynamics rather than being overwhelmed by them.

Integration of Cognitive and Systems-Psychodynamic

The coach connected individual thinking patterns to organisational patterns. Sarah's either/or thinking about profit versus purpose paralleled the board's short-term financial focus. Recognising this connection allowed her to see how shifting her own thinking might influence system-level patterns. This integration helped Sarah recognise how her own cognitive frameworks both reflected and potentially reinforced organisational patterns.

Integration of Gestalt and Existential

The physical positioning exercise connected embodied experience with authentic purpose. Standing in the authentic leadership position created physical feelings of centredness. This embodied experience made the abstract existential concept of authentic leadership feel real. This integration helped Sarah physically experience what authentic purpose feels like, moving it from conceptual understanding to embodied knowing.

Transformative Outcomes

The integrative approach produced several significant shifts for Sarah:

- Physical transformation: From constriction and heaviness to expansiveness and energy
- Cognitive reframing: From either/or thinking to both/and possibilities
- Existential reconnection: From questioning her leadership capability to recommitting to her authentic purpose
- Systemic repositioning: From carrying personal failure to recognising systemic patterns
- Metaphorical shift: From seeing her challenge as "a tangled knot I needed to solve" to "a tapestry I'm helping to weave"

The Coach's Approach

Throughout the session, the coach demonstrated several key capacities essential to integrative coaching:

1. Fluid movement between approaches: Shifting seamlessly between methodologies based on what would best serve Sarah's development in each moment
2. Recognition of interconnections: Seeing how physical experience, thinking patterns, meaning and systemic dynamics were interrelated aspects of Sarah's challenge
3. Appropriate depth regulation: Moving between practical business concerns and deeper existential questions without losing relevance to Sarah's leadership context
4. Integration of being and doing: Addressing both Sarah's inner experience and outer leadership actions
5. Holding complexity: Maintaining awareness of multiple dimensions simultaneously rather than reducing the situation to a single perspective

Conclusion

This integrative executive coaching session demonstrated the power of combining cognitive, Gestalt, existential and systems-psychodynamic approaches. Rather than applying these methodologies sequentially or separately, the coach wove them together into a coherent, multidimensional exploration that addressed Sarah's challenge at multiple levels simultaneously. The result was not merely new insights or strategies but also a fundamental transformation in how Sarah experienced and related to her leadership challenge. By integrating thinking patterns, embodied awareness, authentic purpose and systemic understanding, the session enabled Sarah to access a more centred, expansive and creatively engaged leadership stance in the face of complex competing demands.

The tapestry metaphor that emerged at the end beautifully captured the essence of the integrative approach itself – acknowledging complexity while creating coherence, holding multiple threads while weaving them into a meaningful whole and transforming apparent contradiction into the possibility of lasting value through skilled, patient attention.

Integrative Team Coaching

An integrative coach works with a senior team by synthesising multiple coaching approaches into a comprehensive framework that addresses the full spectrum of team dynamics. Drawing from cognitive, Gestalt, existential and systems-psychodynamic perspectives (among others), the integrative coach can create a multidimensional experience tailored to the team's specific context and challenges.

Rather than applying coaching methodologies sequentially, the integrative coach weaves them together based on what will best serve the team in each moment. For example, when the team is stuck in unproductive thinking patterns, the coach might draw from cognitive approaches to identify mental models and explore alternative perspectives. When tensions or conflicts emerge, the coach might employ Gestalt techniques to bring awareness to present-moment experience and facilitate direct communication. If the team faces difficult choices or a loss of motivation, the coach might use existential approaches to reconnect members with purpose and meaning. And when systemic patterns are affecting team performance, the coach might apply systems-psychodynamic understanding to make unconscious dynamics visible.

The integrative coach can therefore apply this multifaceted approach to address common executive team challenges. Some examples of these may include:

- Strategic Alignment

  For teams struggling with strategic alignment, the coach might use cognitive mapping to make diverse mental models visible (cognitive). They may create experiential exercises where team members physically position themselves to represent strategic priorities (Gestalt) or facilitate dialogue about what truly matters to the organisation and its stakeholders (existential). Or they might explore how organisational history and culture influence current strategic thinking (systems-psychodynamic).
- Decision-Making

  For teams with decision-making challenges, the coach might help identify thinking biases that affect the evaluation of options (cognitive). They may bring awareness to how team members physically and emotionally respond to different alternatives (Gestalt) or connect decisions to core organisational purpose and values (existential). Or they may reveal how unconscious group dynamics might be influencing who holds decision power and authority, formal and informal (systems-psychodynamic).

- Interpersonal Conflict

    For teams experiencing interpersonal conflict, the coach might identify distorted thinking patterns about other team members' intentions (cognitive). They may create experiments that allow direct expression of needs and boundaries (Gestalt) or explore how conflict relates to questions of meaning and authentic leadership (existential). Or they may examine how team members might be carrying projections for the wider system (systems-psychodynamic).

- Organisational Change

    For teams leading change initiatives, the coach might address rigid thinking about what is possible or necessary (cognitive). They may use present-moment awareness to recognise resistance as it emerges (Gestalt) or connect change to deeper purpose and possibilities for authentic contribution (existential). Or they may try to understand anxiety in the system and how the team might be containing it or projecting it (systems-psychodynamic).

- Functional Meetings

    The integrative coach often works with teams during actual working meetings. During these sessions, they may spend time noticing and naming cognitive patterns as they emerge in discussions or bringing awareness to present-moment dynamics – energy shifts, emotional responses, physical positioning etc. They may focus on connecting immediate discussions to the core purpose and meaning, or on identifying systemic patterns playing out in the meeting.

During or after the meeting, the coach can facilitate structured reflection exercises that integrate these multiple perspectives, such as asking the team:

- How are we thinking about this situation? (Cognitive)
- What are we experiencing right now? (Gestalt)
- What matters most in this context? (Existential)
- What might be happening beneath the surface of our team dynamics? (Systems-psychodynamic)

Beyond solving specific problems, the integrative coach can develop the team's capacity to recognise and shift their own thinking patterns (cognitive flexibility), maintain awareness of their present experience together (relational presence), connect to purpose amidst complexity and pressure (existential clarity), or work effectively with unconscious dynamics (systemic intelligence).

The integrative coach helps the team connect their development to broader organisational outcomes by applying new thinking patterns to real business challenges (cognitive), bringing enhanced presence and contact to stakeholder relationships (Gestalt), expressing authentic purpose through strategic and operational decisions (existential) and by influencing systemic patterns throughout the organisation (systems-psychodynamic).

The coach can also ensure that learning transfers beyond the coaching relationship by creating team practices that integrate insights from multiple perspectives. Also, by developing shared language that acknowledges cognitive, experiential, existential, and systemic dimensions, designing decision processes that incorporate multiple ways of knowing and building reflection habits that maintain multilevel awareness.

Summary

The integrative approach to executive team coaching creates a rich, multidimensional experience that acknowledges the complexity of modern leadership. By weaving together the various coaching approaches, the coach helps teams develop greater awareness, effectiveness and cohesion. Rather than offering simplistic solutions, the integrative coach engages with the full spectrum of team dynamics – thinking patterns, present experience, meaningful purpose and systemic forces. This comprehensive approach enables executive teams to navigate complex challenges while developing sustainable capacities for ongoing growth and impact.

Through this integrated work, executive teams can achieve not just improved performance but also a deeper transformation in how they think, relate, find meaning and function as part of larger systems – creating sustainable performance that continues to evolve long after the formal coaching relationship concludes.

Case Study: *Scientific Promise Meets Operational Reality*

Vertex Biosciences, a growing biotech company, stands at a critical inflection point. Their lead immunotherapy candidate, VTX-273, has shown remarkable results in early trials for treatment-resistant cancers, receiving regulatory breakthrough designation and creating significant market expectations.

What began as a small research-focused organisation has rapidly evolved into a mid-sized company balancing scientific discovery with commercial imperatives. This evolution has brought together a diverse leadership team: Katherine Close (CEO), bringing pharmaceutical experience; Dr. James Wilcox (CSO and founder), guarding scientific integrity; Marcus Bailey (Head of Operations), building manufacturing capacity; Elena Rodriguez (Commercial), Sarah Whitman (Finance) and Dr. David Park (Regulatory), rounding out the executive team.

The team now faces a crucial decision that crystallises the tension between scientific caution and operational necessity. Their therapy's production process works for clinical trials but requires significant modification for commercial scale. The scientific team, led by Dr. Wilcox, advocates for an incremental approach to preserve the therapy's efficacy profile. The operations team under Bailey argues for a fundamental redesign of the manufacturing process to ensure reliable commercial production.

This seemingly technical disagreement has surfaced deeper tensions about the company's evolving identity. With scientific roots but commercial ambitions, the organisation struggles to integrate these perspectives. The polarisation along functional lines threatens not just this decision but also the company's ability to navigate future challenges.

Recognising these dynamics, Katherine engaged Carl Reyes, an integrative executive coach, to help the team work through these multidimensional tensions. With a board presentation looming and patients' lives potentially hanging in the balance, how the team resolves this manufacturing challenge will impact both Vertix's future and the accessibility of a potentially life-saving treatment.

An Integrative Team Coaching Session

The leadership team of Vertix Biosciences filed into the conference room, the atmosphere charged with a combination of anticipation and unspoken tension. The company stood at a critical inflection point – their lead immunotherapy candidate showed remarkable promise in early trials, but scaling production while preparing for Phase III trials had created significant strain across the organisation.

Carl Reyes, the integrative executive coach who had been working with the team for three months, observed their arrival with careful attention. CEO Katherine Close entered first, her typically confident stride measured, followed by Dr. James Wilcox, Chief Scientific Officer, who deliberately chose a seat that maintained distance from Marcus Bailey, Head of Operations. Elena Rodriguez, Chief Commercial Officer, positioned herself where she could observe everyone's faces, while Sarah Whitman, Chief Financial Officer, kept her attention on her tablet as she settled in. Dr. David Park, Head of Regulatory Affairs, was the last to arrive, his expression carefully neutral.

"I appreciate everyone making time for our session today," Carl began once they had gathered. "Based on our individual conversations over the past week, it's clear the manufacturing scale-up challenges have surfaced some significant tensions in how you're working together. Today, we'll approach these challenges using multiple perspectives to deepen understanding and create new possibilities." He gestured to the whiteboard where he had written four dimensions of exploration: Thinking Patterns, Present Experience, Purpose and Meaning, and Systemic Dynamics.

"Katherine, would you like to frame the current situation from your perspective?" Carl invited.

Katherine straightened in her chair. "We're facing a critical manufacturing decision. Our current process yields enough product for clinical trials, but scaling to commercial levels will require significant modifications. James and his team believe we should optimise the current process incrementally, while Marcus recommends a more fundamental redesign of the manufacturing approach." Her voice tightening slightly, "The board expects a recommendation next week. James believes Marcus's approach risks changing the product profile. Marcus believes James is being unnecessarily cautious. Meanwhile, Elena is concerned about timelines for commercial planning, Sarah is worried about capital expenditures, and David sees regulatory risks in both approaches. We're stuck."

Carl nodded. "Thank you for that clear overview. Rather than immediately diving into the technical details, I'd like us to explore the multiple dimensions of this challenge." He turned to the team. "First, I'm curious about the thinking patterns that might be influencing how each of you is approaching this decision."

James, the CSO, responded first. "I'm operating from a risk-minimisation framework. We have promising clinical data with the current process. Any significant change introduces variables that could affect efficacy or safety. The science says: don't mess with what's working."

Marcus nodded but then countered, "I understand that perspective, but I'm thinking about scalability and long-term sustainability. The current process works at small scale but has fundamental limitations for commercial production. I'm applying systems thinking – optimising the whole rather than protecting individual components."

"These are different but equally valid cognitive frameworks," Carl observed, making notes on the whiteboard under "Thinking Patterns." "James is using a protection-of-assets mental model while Marcus is applying a systems optimisation framework. Both have merit depending on the context." He turned to the others. "What thinking patterns are informing your perspectives?"

Elena shared that she was using a market-readiness timeline framework, Sarah described a capital efficiency model and David explained his risk-regulation balance approach. As each person spoke, Carl mapped their cognitive frameworks visually.

"What's emerging here is fascinating," he noted. "You're all using rigorous thinking processes, but they're based on different priorities and assumptions. None are wrong, but they're not being integrated effectively." Carl then shifted to a more Gestalt-oriented approach. "Now I'd like to explore what's happening in your present experience as we discuss this challenge. What are you noticing in your body, your emotions, and your interactions right now?"

The question created a momentary silence, the team unaccustomed to this dimension of awareness.

"I notice I'm sitting forward, almost braced for conflict," Katherine admitted. "There's tension across my shoulders and a knot in my stomach."

"I'm aware that I haven't made eye contact with Marcus since we started," James acknowledged. "And my jaw is tight, which happens when I'm feeling defensive."

"I'm positioned as if I'm about to jump in and mediate," Elena observed. "It's physically uncomfortable but completely habitual."

As each team member shared their immediate awareness, Carl guided them to notice both their physical presence and the quality of contact they were making with themselves and others. He observed aloud how some were making direct eye contact while others were looking at the table or middle distance. He also noticed that some were fully occupying their chairs, while others were perched at the edges. "This present-moment awareness is valuable data," Carl noted. "Your bodies are expressing tensions and patterns that might not be fully conscious."

He then introduced an existential dimension. "Let's connect to the deeper purpose that brought each of you to this work. Beyond the immediate manufacturing decision, what matters most to you about Vertix's mission and your role in it?"

The quality of attention in the room shifted noticeably with this question.

"What matters most to me is getting this therapy to patients who have no other options," James said quietly. "I've watched too many people fail on existing treatments. Everything else is secondary to maintaining the efficacy we've seen so far."

Marcus nodded with unexpected emotion. "I share that purpose completely. My focus on manufacturing redesign is about ensuring we can reliably deliver this therapy to every patient who needs it, not just the few hundred in our trials."

One by one, each team member connected to the deeper purpose driving their work. Despite their different approaches, a common thread emerged – a genuine commitment to transforming treatment for patients facing limited options.

"Notice how the energy in the room has shifted as you've connected to shared purpose," Carl observed. "This existential dimension – the meaning you find in your work – provides a foundation for working through your different perspectives."

Carl then brought in a systems-psychodynamic lens. "Now I'd like to explore the systemic dynamics that might be influencing how you're working together. How might organisational history, roles, or unconscious patterns be shaping your interactions?"

Katherine considered this thoughtfully. "Vertix was founded by scientists, with scientific rigor as our core identity. As we've grown and brought in operational and commercial expertise, there's been an unconscious hierarchy with science at the top. I wonder if that's making it harder for non-scientific perspectives to be fully valued."

"That resonates," Marcus acknowledged. "Sometimes I feel I have to work twice as hard to have my operational expertise recognised compared to scientific input."

"And I notice that as the company approaches commercialisation, there's anxiety about what it means to become a 'commercial' organisation," Elena added. "Almost as if we fear losing our scientific soul."

David, who had been relatively quiet, spoke up. "There's also a pattern where Regulatory gets positioned as the obstacle rather than a strategic partner. I sometimes feel like I'm cast as the person who says 'no' when I'm actually trying to create pathways to 'yes.'"

As these systemic patterns emerged, Carl mapped them on the whiteboard, helping the team see how their current manufacturing decision was embedded in larger organisational dynamics. "These systemic forces are powerful but often invisible," he noted. "By recognising them, you can work with them consciously rather than being unconsciously driven by them."

Having explored these multiple dimensions, Carl invited the team to integrate these perspectives through an experiential exercise. "I'd like you to physically arrange yourselves in the room to represent your current approach to the manufacturing decision," he suggested. "Position yourselves in a way that shows your relationships to each other and to the decision."

After a moment's consideration, the team members stood and began arranging themselves. James and Marcus positioned themselves on opposite sides of the room. Katherine stood between them but slightly removed, as if trying to maintain a connection to both while not fully aligned with either. Elena, Sarah and David formed a loose cluster apart from the central dynamic, observing but not fully engaged.

"Take a moment to notice this configuration," Carl said. "What does it reveal about how you're approaching this challenge?"

"We're polarised," Sarah observed. "And the three of us who aren't directly involved in the technical disagreement have essentially removed ourselves from the process."

"I'm physically trying to maintain connection to both positions without fully committing," Katherine realised. "That's probably creating more uncertainty for everyone."

Carl nodded. "Now I'd like you to experiment with a physical arrangement that might better support an integrated approach to this decision. Move intentionally, noticing what shifts inside you as you change positions."

The team members began to move. James and Marcus took several steps towards each other, reducing the distance while maintaining their distinct positions. Katherine moved to form a triangle with them rather than standing between them. Elena, Sarah and David moved to join this central configuration, each positioning themselves to connect with multiple perspectives rather than remaining observers.

"What's different in this arrangement?" Carl asked.

"We've maintained our distinct perspectives but reduced the polarisation," James noted. "And everyone is part of a single configuration rather than separate groups."

"I can see everyone's faces now," Marcus added. "In the previous arrangement, I couldn't make eye contact with half the team without turning my back on others."

"There's more possibility in this configuration," Katherine observed. "We're not aligned yet, but at least we can see and hear each other more fully."

Carl invited them to return to their seats, carrying this embodied experience with them. As they settled back around the table, there was a subtle but distinct shift in their presence – more direct eye contact and more relaxed postures and engagement.

"Now let's integrate these different perspectives to approach your manufacturing decision in a new way," Carl suggested. "How might you honour the various thinking patterns, present experiences, shared purpose, and systemic dynamics we've explored?"

This prompted a rich discussion where the team began crafting an integrated approach. They acknowledged the validity of both risk minimisation and systems optimisation thinking frameworks, creating space for both perspectives in their decision process. They agreed to pay attention to their physical and emotional responses during technical discussions, recognising these as valuable data. They recommitted to their shared purpose of serving patients, using this as a touchstone for evaluating options. They identified ways to work with, rather than against systemic patterns, including explicitly valuing diverse expertise and reframing Regulatory's role as a strategic partner. As practical next steps, they also designed a decision-making approach that incorporated a joint evaluation team with equal representation from Science and Operations. Explicit criteria reflecting both scientific and operational priorities, regular check-ins on the emotional and interpersonal dimensions of the process, connection to patient impact as the ultimate decision criterion, and awareness of how organisational history and identity were influencing perspectives.

"What I notice now," Carl observed as they finalised their approach, "is a different quality of engagement compared to when we started. You're still holding different perspectives, but you're doing so within a shared framework rather than as competing positions."

Katherine nodded. "This doesn't make the technical challenges any easier, but it does create a foundation for working through them together rather than against each other."

"I feel like we've moved from defending positions to exploring possibilities," James acknowledged, making direct eye contact with Marcus for the first time in the session.

"And from fragmentation to some genuine integration," Marcus added with a nod of recognition.

As the session concluded, Carl summarised the multiple dimensions they had explored. "Today you've examined your thinking patterns, becoming aware of different mental models that were operating implicitly. You've increased your present-moment awareness, noticing how tensions and possibilities were manifesting physically and emotionally. You've connected to shared purpose and meaning that transcends your immediate disagreements. And you've recognised systemic patterns that were influencing your interactions in ways you hadn't fully acknowledged." He continued, "The approach you've designed doesn't eliminate the complexity of your manufacturing decision, but it does create a more integrated container for working with that complexity. By holding multiple perspectives simultaneously, you've opened up possibilities that weren't visible when you were operating from fragmented viewpoints."

As the team prepared to leave, Carl observed the subtle but meaningful shifts in how they moved and interacted – James and Marcus exchanging ideas about next steps, Elena engaging David in a conversation about regulatory strategy as it related to commercial planning, and Sarah and Katherine discussing how to communicate their approach to the board.

The manufacturing decision remained challenging, but the team had discovered a more integrated way of approaching it – one that honoured the cognitive, experiential, existential and systemic dimensions of their work together. In doing so, they had not just addressed an immediate business challenge but also had developed new capacities for collaborative leadership that would serve them through the many complex decisions that still lay ahead.

Analysing the Session

This coaching session with the Vertix leadership team exemplifies integrative coaching at its most effective – weaving together multiple coaching perspectives to create a multidimensional approach that addresses the full spectrum of team dynamics. Let's analyse what transpired from an integrative coaching perspective:

Integrating Multiple Coaching Frameworks

The strength of Carl Reyes's integrative approach lies in his deliberate synthesis of our four distinct coaching methodologies:

Cognitive Framework Integration

Carl begins by explicitly mapping the different thinking patterns team members bring to the manufacturing decision, including:

- James's "risk-minimisation framework" focused on protecting clinical efficacy
- Marcus's "systems optimisation framework" focused on scalability
- Elena's "market-readiness timeline framework"
- Sarah's "capital efficiency model"
- David's "risk-regulation balance approach"

Rather than treating these as competing frameworks to choose between, he validates each as "different but equally valid cognitive frameworks" that "all have merit depending on the context." This cognitive mapping creates visibility of mental models that were previously operating implicitly and in opposition.

Gestalt Awareness Integration

Carl then shifts to a Gestalt approach by inviting present-moment awareness, including:

- Katherine notices that she's "sitting forward, almost braced for conflict" with "tension across her shoulders"
- James becomes aware he "hasn't made eye contact with Marcus" and has a "tight jaw"

- Elena recognises her physical positioning "as if I'm about to jump in and mediate"

By bringing attention to immediate physical experience, Carl helps team members recognise how the conflict manifests in their bodies and interactions. This embodied awareness provides data about the tension that purely cognitive approaches might miss.

Existential Purpose Integration

The session deepens significantly when Maya introduces an existential dimension, asking about "the deeper purpose that brought each of you to this work":

- James connects to his purpose of helping "patients who have no other options"
- Marcus reveals his shared commitment to "deliver this therapy to every patient who needs it"

This exploration reveals a profound common ground that transcends their methodological differences. The existential dimension becomes a foundation for integration, as Carl notes: "This existential dimension – the meaning you find in your work – provides a foundation for working through your different perspectives."

Systems-Psychodynamic Understanding Integration

Maya then incorporates systems-psychodynamic insights by exploring "systemic dynamics that might be influencing how you're working together":

- Katherine identifies an "unconscious hierarchy with science at the top"
- Marcus acknowledges feeling his "operational expertise" isn't equally valued
- Elena notes anxiety about becoming a "commercial organisation" and losing their "scientific soul"
- David describes how "Regulatory gets positioned as the obstacle"

This systems-level awareness helps the team see how their manufacturing disagreement is embedded in larger organisational patterns and unconscious dynamics.

Experiential Integration

The session's transformative moment comes through an experiential exercise that physically embodies the team's dynamics, when team members position themselves to represent their current approach:

- James and Marcus stand "on opposite sides of the room"
- Katherine positions herself "between them but slightly removed"
- Elena, Sarah and David form "a loose cluster apart from the central dynamic"

This physical representation makes visible what Sarah observes as polarisation and Katherine recognises as her attempt to "maintain connection to both positions without fully committing."

The team then experiments with a new physical arrangement:

- James and Marcus "took several steps toward each other."
- Katherine moves to "form a triangle with them rather than standing between them."
- Elena, Sarah and David "join this central configuration."

This physical reconfiguration creates immediate shifts in perspective, with Marcus noting, "I can see everyone's faces now," and Katherine observing "more possibility in this configuration."

The power of this experiential integration is how it simultaneously addresses cognitive patterns (seeing multiple perspectives), Gestalt awareness (immediate physical experience), existential purpose (connecting around shared commitment) and systems dynamics (reconfiguring the organisational pattern).

Integrated Outcomes

The session ends by producing several integrated outcomes that would be unlikely from any single coaching approach, including the design of a decision-making approach that incorporates:

1. Cognitive integration: "Both risk-minimisation and systems-optimisation thinking frameworks"
2. Gestalt awareness: "Attention to physical and emotional responses during technical discussions"
3. Existential purpose: "Connection to patient impact as the ultimate decision criterion"
4. Systems understanding: "Awareness of how organisational history and identity were influencing perspectives"

By the session's end, there are visible changes in how team members relate. These shifts represent integration at the relational level – not just intellectual understanding but also transformed quality of contact. Carl's summary highlights the multidimensional nature of what the team has accomplished, emphasising that their approach "doesn't eliminate the complexity" but "creates a more integrated container for working with that complexity."

The Coach's Integrative Stance

Throughout the session, Carl demonstrates several key capacities essential to integrative coaching, including fluid movement between the different methodologies. He shifts seamlessly between different coaching approaches based on what would serve the team's development in each moment. For example, he begins with cognitive mapping to create visibility of thinking patterns. He then shifts to Gestalt awareness when embodied understanding is needed. He introduces existential purpose when a deeper connection would serve integration, and finally, he brings in systems-psychodynamic perspectives to address organisational patterns. These transitions aren't arbitrary but follow a developmental logic, building from awareness to possibility.

Carl also demonstrates keen awareness of what coaching approach would best serve in each moment. He begins with cognitive mapping because the team's initial polarisation is based on conflicting mental models. He then introduces Gestalt awareness when cognitive understanding alone isn't creating movement. He brings in existential purpose precisely when the team needs a foundation for integration, and finally, he explores systems dynamics when the team is ready to see beyond immediate conflict.

Throughout the session, Carl models the integration he seeks to develop, and this multidimensional presence creates the foundation that supports the team's own integration work.

Conclusion

This session exemplifies effective integrative coaching – not as a random collection of techniques but as a coherent, multidimensional approach that addresses the full spectrum of human and organisational experience. By weaving together cognitive, Gestalt, existential and systems-psychodynamic perspectives, Carl helps the Vertix team move from polarisation to integration, from fragmentation to cohesion.

The manufacturing decision remains technically complex, but the team now has a more integrated container for working with that complexity. More importantly, they've developed new capacities for collaborative leadership that will serve them through future challenges – the ability to recognise different thinking patterns, maintain present-moment awareness, connect to shared purpose and work consciously with systemic dynamics.

This integration represents not just a better way to make this particular decision but also a transformative shift in how the team functions together – one that serves both their differences and their common ground, both their individual perspectives and their collective purpose.

Chapter 15

The Importance of the Coaching Relationship

The coaching relationship stands as the foundational element upon which all effective coaching is built. More than just a context for coaching techniques or a vehicle for delivering interventions, the relationship between coach and client is itself a primary mechanism of change and development. Research consistently shows that the quality of this relationship is one of the strongest predictors of coaching outcomes and often more significant than the specific coaching methodology employed.

The Coaching Relationship as a Container for Development

The coaching relationship provides psychological safety – a space where clients can explore vulnerabilities, examine blind spots and experiment with new ways of thinking and being without fear of judgement or negative consequences. This safety is crucial because meaningful development often requires venturing into uncomfortable territory, questioning long-held assumptions and acknowledging limitations.

When clients feel safe with their coach, they can:

- Share thoughts and feelings they might censor elsewhere
- Acknowledge mistakes and failures as learning opportunities
- Explore contradictions in their thinking or behaviour
- Reveal aspirations that might seem unrealistic or inappropriate in other contexts
- Express emotions that might be suppressed in organisational settings

This psychological safety doesn't happen automatically but is carefully cultivated through the coach's consistent demonstration of respect, confidentiality, non-judgement and genuine positive regard.

Establishing trust is the foundation on which psychological safety is built and forms the bedrock of the coaching relationship. Clients must trust that:

- The coach has their best interests at heart
- Their vulnerabilities won't be exploited

DOI: 10.4324/9781003594215-20

- The coach is competent to facilitate their development
- Confidentiality will be maintained
- The coach will provide honest feedback even when uncomfortable

This trust develops over time through reliability, consistency, appropriate transparency, demonstrated competence and the maintenance of clear boundaries. High-trust relationships permit deeper exploration and more significant risk-taking, both essential for transformative development.

The Coaching Relationship as a Developmental Process

The coaching relationship offers clients a unique reflective experience that is rarely available elsewhere. The coach reflects patterns, inconsistencies, strengths and blind spots that the client might not otherwise perceive. This reflection is not just intellectual feedback; it can also include:

- Observations about emotional patterns
- Recognition of incongruence between stated values and actions
- Awareness of habitual responses to challenges
- Identification of unexamined assumptions
- Noticeable shifts in energy, engagement or presence

This reflection is key in helping clients develop greater self-awareness – a cornerstone of leadership effectiveness.

Developmental psychologists have demonstrated that adult development requires certain types of relationships that can both support and challenge existing ways of making meaning. The coaching relationship can serve this developmental function by both supporting and challenging the client's current capacities and perspectives; that is,

- Constructively challenging limiting assumptions and frameworks, and introducing more complex ways of understanding situations
- Providing scaffolding for the development of new capacities by offering a secure base from which to explore new territory

Unlike many professional relationships that primarily focus on performance, the coaching relationship explicitly aims to facilitate the client's growth and development (which then, in turn, leads to an enhancement in performance).

The Impact of Positive Regard

The coach's consistent demonstration of what Carl Rogers called "unconditional positive regard" – valuing the client as a whole person regardless of specific behaviours or achievements – creates a unique relational dynamic that supports growth.

This is not about approving everything the client does, but rather about respecting the client's autonomy and agency and believing in their capacity for positive development. It is about holding a compassionate understanding of difficulties and limitations while maintaining faith in their potential, even when the client may doubt themselves.

This positive regard creates a relational environment where clients feel worthy of growth and capable of change, countering the self-doubt that can often limit development.

Working with Transference and Countertransference

The coaching relationship inevitably activates relational patterns from the client's past and present. While coaching is not therapy, being aware of these patterns can provide valuable leverage for development. For example, clients may relate to coaches in ways that mirror how they relate to authority figures in their own organisations, and responses to the coach's challenges or support can reveal patterns in how clients habitually handle feedback. Also, the client's interpretation of the coach's actions may reveal projection patterns, and expectations of the coach may illuminate their unconscious expectations of others.

Skilled coaches recognise these patterns and, when appropriate, use them as data to help clients gain insight into their relational tendencies and blind spots. It remains to be seen what will happen to this important psychological phenomenon with the introduction of AI coach-bots.

Creating Conditions for Effective Challenge

The strength of the coaching relationship determines how much challenge a client can productively absorb. Without a solid relationship, challenges may be experienced as criticism or attack rather than as opportunities for growth. With a strong relationship, the coach can ask more difficult questions, and inconsistencies can be pointed out more directly. Also, limiting beliefs and hidden assumptions can be challenged and examined more explicitly, and uncomfortable feedback can be shared more candidly.

Research suggests that the optimal balance of support and challenge leads to the greatest development, but this balance depends entirely on the coaching client and the quality of the coaching relationship.

Enabling Experimentation and Risk-Taking

A strong coaching relationship can create conditions where clients feel secure enough to experiment with new behaviours, approaches and ways of thinking. This security allows for testing unfamiliar leadership styles, making decisions from different perspectives, exploring vulnerability when appropriate and revealing authentic concerns or aspirations.

This experimentation is essential for development because sustainable change requires not just insight but also practical experience with new ways of being and leading.

Phases of the Coaching Relationship

The coaching relationship typically evolves through distinct phases, each with its own relational dynamics and developmental possibilities:

1. Formation: Establishing trust, clarifying expectations, beginning to build understanding
2. Deepening: Developing greater openness, taking more interpersonal risks, building trust through experience
3. Working: Engaging with core challenges, navigating resistance, leveraging the relationship for development
4. Integration: Consolidating learning, transferring insights to other relationships, preparing for conclusion
5. Closure: Acknowledging the impact of the relationship, celebrating growth, establishing post-coaching connection

Skilled coaches are attentive to these relational phases and adjust their approach accordingly, recognising that different interventions are appropriate at different stages of the relationship.

All of these capacities are developed through personal reflection, supervision and ongoing professional development.

Conclusion

The coaching relationship is not merely the context where coaching happens – it is itself a primary mechanism of development. When clients experience a relationship characterised by safety, trust, appropriate challenge and positive regard, they gain access to developmental possibilities that remain unavailable in less intentional relationships. The coaching relationship becomes both a container for growth and a laboratory for experimenting with new ways of relating – to oneself, to others and to the challenges of leadership and life more broadly. By recognising the central importance of the coaching relationship, coaches can move beyond technique-focused approaches to create truly transformative developmental partnerships with their clients.

Chapter 16

The Importance of Coach Development

The practice of coaching, particularly when spanning existential, systems psychodynamic, gestalt and cognitive approaches with both individuals and teams, demands an extraordinary level of development from the coach. Far beyond mere technical competence or methodological familiarity, this work requires coaches to engage in continuous, deep personal and professional development that transforms not just what they know but also who they are. The developmental journey of such coaches must be as multidimensional and integrated as the coaching they provide. And here's why:

Coach as Instrument

At the heart of coaching practice lies a fundamental reality: the coach themselves serves as the primary instrument of their work. Unlike professions where practitioners can rely primarily on external tools, methodologies or technologies, coaches work primarily through their presence, awareness and relational capacity. This reality makes the development of the coach as a person inseparable from their development as a professional. For example, a coach working with systems psychodynamic principles must develop their own capacity to recognise and work with unconscious material. A coach employing Gestalt approaches must cultivate heightened present-moment awareness in themselves. A coach utilising existential frameworks must engage deeply with questions of values, meaning and purpose in their own life. And a coach applying cognitive approaches must develop sophisticated metacognitive awareness of their own thinking patterns.

A coach's ability to navigate fluidly between any or all of these approaches depends on having personally experienced and integrated them in their own development. Without this embodied integration, coaches risk the mechanical application of techniques without the presence and authenticity that make coaching transformative. Leaders and teams quickly sense when a coach is operating from memorised techniques versus embodied wisdom. The coach's own developmental journey, therefore, becomes the foundation upon which all their methodological expertise rests.

DOI: 10.4324/9781003594215-21

Developmental Breadth and Depth

The breadth of development required for effective coaching is uniquely demanding. Coaches must develop across multiple dimensions simultaneously: cognitive complexity, emotional intelligence, somatic awareness, relational capacity, systemic understanding and existential depth. Cognitive development alone, while necessary, can prove wholly insufficient. Coaches need to develop the emotional range to work with the full spectrum of human experience that emerges in coaching relationships. They require somatic development to recognise and work with embodied patterns in themselves and their clients. They must develop relational capacities that allow them to create psychological safety while offering challenging observations. Their systemic awareness needs development to recognise patterns and dynamics beyond individual behaviour. And they need existential depth to engage with the profound questions of meaning and purpose that emerge, particularly at senior leadership levels.

This multidimensional development cannot remain compartmentalised but must itself become integrated within the coach. Just as they help clients integrate different aspects of experience, coaches must continuously work towards greater integration of their own cognitive, emotional, somatic, relational, systemic and existential dimensions. This integration allows them to respond fluidly to whatever emerges in coaching conversations, drawing from the most appropriate approach without artificial shifts between modalities.

Self-as-Instrument Development

Coaches need this depth of ongoing development to enable them to use themselves effectively as instruments of change:

- Presence development – forms the foundation of effective coaching across all approaches. Coaches must cultivate the capacity to be fully present with whatever emerges in the coaching relationship, neither overwhelmed by intensity nor disconnected from difficulty. This presence allows them to create a container for development that clients experience as both challenging and supportive. Presence involves practices that enhance attentional stability, emotional regulation and embodied awareness.
- Perceptual development – also expands coaches' capacity to perceive patterns at multiple levels simultaneously. Skilled coaches perceive not just explicit content but also tone, body language, emotional undercurrents, systemic patterns and existential themes. This multilevel perception allows them to recognise which approach might best serve in a particular moment. Perceptual development involves continuously refining observational skills across sensory, emotional, cognitive and intuitive channels.
- Relational development – is also fundamental, as it enhances the coaches' ability to form effective developmental relationships with a diverse spectrum of

clients. Coaches must connect authentically with analytical executives who prefer cognitive approaches, emotionally expressive leaders who respond to gestalt work, systems-oriented teams needing psychodynamic perspectives and those facing existential questions about meaning and purpose. This relational range doesn't mean becoming chameleon-like but rather developing sufficient flexibility to establish genuine connection across different relational styles.

- Personal edge development – involves coaches continuously working with their own limitations, triggers and growth edges. Coaches inevitably encounter situations that activate their own unresolved issues or developmental challenges, and their effectiveness depends not on having resolved all personal issues (an impossible standard) but on their capacity to recognise when they're triggered and maintain effectiveness despite activation. This development requires ongoing self-reflection, personal therapy or coaching and courageous engagement with their own developmental edges.

The Reflective Practitioner Stance

Beyond specific capacities, coaches must develop a fundamental stance as reflective practitioners – continuously examining their work with curious, non-defensive attention. This stance includes rigorous reflection on why they choose particular interventions, what patterns emerge across their coaching relationships, where they feel most competent and most challenged and how their personal history influences their coaching preferences. Without this reflective stance, coaches risk falling into habitual patterns or methodological biases rather than truly responding to client needs.

Such reflective practice requires structured approaches, including regular supervision with experienced mentor coaches, peer consultation with colleagues who can offer different perspectives, systematic review of coaching sessions, ongoing client feedback and dedicated reflection time built into professional practice. The most effective coaches treat their own development with the same seriousness and commitment they bring to client work, recognising that the depth of their impact correlates directly with the depth of their own development.

Vertical Development Requirements

Coaching, particularly at senior leadership levels, requires not just horizontal development (expanding knowledge and skills) but also vertical development (transforming meaning-making capacity and perspective). Coaches working with complex organisational dynamics and senior leadership challenges need to have developed sufficient cognitive complexity, perspective-taking capacity, systems awareness and comfort with paradox to meet the developmental demands of their work. Research on adult development suggests that coaches need to have developed at least to the level of complexity they hope to facilitate in their clients, and preferably beyond that level.

This vertical development isn't achieved through training programmes or skill acquisition alone but requires transformative experiences that challenge and expand the coach's meaning-making systems. Such development typically involves a combination of structured developmental programmes, challenging work experiences, significant life transitions, deep reflective practice and ongoing developmental relationships with mentors operating at more complex developmental levels.

Professional Knowledge Development

Alongside personal development, coaches need continuous development of their own professional knowledge across multiple domains:

- Theoretical understanding – must span diverse fields, including adult development theory, systems theory, group dynamics, psychodynamic concepts, existential philosophy, cognitive science, organisational behaviour and leadership theory. This theoretical foundation provides conceptual frameworks for making sense of the complex phenomena coaches encounter in their work.
- Methodological expertise – must develop across the full range of coaching approaches, with deep understanding of when and how to apply (in our example) existential, systems psychodynamic, Gestalt and cognitive methods with both individuals and teams. This expertise includes fluency with specific interventions, recognition of contraindications and skill in transitioning between approaches when appropriate.
- Contextual knowledge – must continuously expand through ongoing learning about business trends, organisational models, industry dynamics, cultural differences and contemporary leadership challenges. Without this contextual understanding, coaches risk applying sophisticated methodologies in ways disconnected from the real-world circumstances their clients navigate.

The coach commits to being a perpetual student, recognising that the complexity of their work demands continuous expansion of their knowledge and themselves across almost all domains.

Ethical Development

Perhaps most fundamentally, coaches need ongoing ethical development that enables them to navigate the complex boundary issues, power dynamics, competing stakeholder interests and potential role conflicts inherent in sophisticated coaching work. Coaches need to develop:

- Ethical discernment – that goes beyond rule-following to wise navigation of complex situations where different values may come into tension. This discernment develops through regular ethical reflection, consultation on challenging cases and thoughtful examination of past ethical dilemmas.

- Boundary clarity – about their role, limitations, appropriate commitments and the distinctions between coaching and other professional relationships. This clarity prevents role confusion and helps coaches maintain appropriate focus in their work.
- Courage – to address difficult issues directly, to say no when appropriate, to acknowledge mistakes and to prioritise client welfare over other considerations, including financial incentives or reputation enhancement. This ethical courage develops through conscious practice and reflection on situations that challenge the coach's ethical resolve.

Holistic Approaches to Coach Development

Given these multifaceted development requirements, effective coach development requires holistic approaches that address the full spectrum of developmental needs. Formal education and certification in multiple coaching methodologies provide a necessary but insufficient foundation for coaching. While valuable, such training must be complemented by broader development. Ongoing supervision offers crucial support for coaches, providing spaces to explore countertransference, methodological questions, ethical dilemmas and developmental edges with experienced mentor coaches. Regular supervision should be considered non-negotiable for coaches working at this level of complexity. Additionally, personal therapy or coaching provides coaches with firsthand experience of the methodologies they use, while also addressing their own developmental needs. Coaches who have experienced powerful coaching themselves bring a deeper understanding to their work with others.

Continuous client work, along with systematic reflection, provides essential developmental opportunities. Each coaching engagement offers rich learning when approached with genuine curiosity and rigorous reflection rather than the habitual application of familiar approaches. Learning communities can also connect coaches with colleagues for case consultation, mutual learning and exposure to diverse perspectives. These communities counteract the isolation that can occur in coaching practice and provide valuable feedback on blind spots or developmental edges.

Conclusion: Development as a Professional Responsibility

For coaches working across existential, systems psychodynamic, Gestalt and cognitive approaches with both individuals and teams, continuous personal and professional development represents not merely best practice but also a professional responsibility. The complex human systems these coaches serve deserve nothing less than practitioners committed to development as deep and multifaceted as the work itself. The most impactful coaches recognise that their greatest contribution comes not just from what they know or what they do, but also from who they are and how they show up in the coaching relationship. Their ongoing commitment to their own development creates the foundation for truly transformative work with leaders and teams navigating increasingly complex organisational challenges. In this sense, the coach's development journey never ends but continues to unfold alongside their professional practice, each informing and enhancing the other in a continuous cycle of growth and integration.

As coaching continues to evolve as a profession, this commitment to multi-dimensional development distinguishes truly masterful practitioners from those who merely apply techniques. Organisations and leaders seeking transformative coaching experiences would be well-served to enquire not just about a coach's methodological expertise or client experience but also about their ongoing development practices and how they continue to grow as practitioners. The most valuable answer may not be a list of credentials or training programmes but evidence of a lived commitment to development as profound and integrated as the coaching they offer.

The field of coaching continues to evolve rapidly, with new research, methodologies and applications continuously emerging. Coaches who fail to develop risk having their approaches become outdated or their effectiveness diminished as client needs and contexts continue to change.

Chapter 17

The Evolving Coaching Landscape

As we conclude our exploration of coaching approaches, it seems fitting to pause and consider both the current landscape of coaching practice and its potential future trajectories. The field of coaching has undergone a remarkable evolution over the past few decades – from its early roots in sports psychology and management consulting to its current status as a sophisticated profession addressing the multidimensional nature of human development in organisational contexts. This final chapter examines the state of coaching today and considers where it might be headed in the coming years.

Professionalisation and Standardisation

One of the most significant developments in the coaching field has been its movement towards greater professionalisation. Organisations like the International Coaching Federation, the European Mentoring and Coaching Council, the Association for Coaching and, more recently, the British Psychological Society have established competency frameworks, ethical guidelines and accreditation processes that have helped transform coaching from an unregulated activity into a recognised profession with defined standards. This professionalisation has not only brought increased credibility but also raised important questions about the balance between standardisation and methodological diversity. As we've seen throughout this book, different coaching approaches offer distinct value. The challenge for professional bodies is to maintain standards while honouring the rich diversity of effective coaching approaches.

Research and Evidence Base

The evidence base for coaching effectiveness has grown substantially in recent years. Meta-analyses and systematic reviews consistently demonstrate positive effects of coaching on performance, well-being, coping, work attitudes and goal-directed self-regulation, and increasingly sophisticated research designs have strengthened these findings. However, research comparing the effectiveness of different coaching approaches remains limited. Most studies examine coaching as a

DOI: 10.4324/9781003594215-22

general intervention rather than investigating the specific contributions of existential, systems psychodynamic, gestalt, cognitive, or other approaches. This gap presents an important opportunity for future research that could inform more targeted applications of different methodologies.

Expanding Applications

While this book has focused primarily on leadership and team coaching in organisational settings, coaching applications have expanded considerably beyond these contexts. Health coaching supports behaviour change for improved well-being. Life coaching addresses personal development and goal achievement outside work contexts. Career coaching helps individuals navigate increasingly complex professional landscapes. Peer coaching creates developmental partnerships between colleagues. Each of these domains has developed specialised approaches tailored to specific needs and contexts. Within organisations, coaching has also expanded beyond traditional executive coaching to include team coaching, group coaching and "leader as coach" approaches that embed coaching principles into management practice. This expansion reflects growing recognition of coaching's value at multiple organisational levels.

Integration with Related Fields

Contemporary coaching increasingly integrates insights from adjacent fields, including positive psychology, neuroscience, adult development theory and systems thinking. This cross-disciplinary integration has enriched coaching practice with new concepts, tools and perspectives. The boundaries between coaching and related helping professions – including therapy, consulting, mentoring and training – have become more nuanced as practitioners recognise both the distinct and the complementary aspects of each of these modalities. Many professionals now work across these boundaries, adapting their approach to client needs while maintaining appropriate role clarity.

Technological Mediation

The coaching relationship, traditionally conducted in person, has increasingly moved to virtual formats – a trend dramatically accelerated by the global pandemic. Video coaching sessions have become normalised, and research suggests that well-conducted virtual coaching can be as effective as in-person coaching for many applications. Beyond video sessions, digital coaching platforms now offer scaled coaching solutions, sometimes combined with AI-driven tools that provide additional support between human coaching interactions. These technological developments have made coaching more accessible while raising important questions about the essential elements of effective coaching relationships.

Emerging Trends and Future Directions

As we look towards the future of coaching, several significant trends and potential developments merit consideration.

Towards Greater Integration

The integrative coaching approach described in the latter chapters of this book represents a broader trend in the field and a movement away from rigid methodological boundaries towards more flexible, multidimensional practice. Future coaching seems likely to continue this integration, with practitioners drawing from diverse theoretical frameworks while maintaining coherent, principled approaches tailored to specific contexts and needs. This integration extends beyond coaching methodologies to include a greater connection between individual, systemic and even environmental perspectives. Future coaching practice will likely address individual development, organisational systems and the environment these systems are embedded within, recognising that sustainable change requires attention to all of the dimensions that shape and constrain human behaviour.

Vertical Development Focus

Much coaching has traditionally focused on horizontal development – expanding skills, knowledge and competencies within existing meaning-making systems. However, increasing organisational complexity creates growing demand for vertical development – transformation in how leaders make meaning of their experience, not just what they know. Adult development theories that map the evolution of meaning-making capacity are increasingly informing coaching practice. Future coaching approaches will likely place greater emphasis on facilitating these developmental shifts, particularly for leaders navigating volatile, uncertain, complex and ambiguous challenges that require more sophisticated meaning-making capabilities.

Cultural and Contextual Adaptation

As coaching expands globally, practitioners increasingly recognise the need to adapt approaches for different cultural contexts. Western coaching methodologies often emphasise individual agency, direct communication and personal achievement – values that may not align with more collectivist or relationship-oriented cultures. Future coaching practice will likely develop more sophisticated approaches to cultural adaptation, moving beyond superficial adjustments to deep engagement with diverse worldviews and values.

Collective and Systemic Applications

While individual coaching remains prevalent, future applications will likely expand further into collective and systemic domains. Team coaching approaches continue to mature, addressing not just interpersonal dynamics but also collective cognition, team identity and systemic positioning. Organisation-wide coaching initiatives aim to shift entire cultures rather than just developing individual leaders. These collective applications demand new conceptual frameworks and methodologies that address emergent properties of human systems rather than simply applying individual coaching approaches to groups. The systems psychodynamic perspective described in this book offers valuable foundations for this work, but new integrative approaches for collective coaching continue to emerge.

Technological Transformation

Perhaps the most disruptive potential changes involve technology's role in coaching. Several technological developments warrant particular attention.

Artificial Intelligence in Coaching – AI-enhanced coaching platforms are already appearing, offering algorithmically driven guidance based on data analysis and pattern recognition. While unlikely to replace human coaching for complex developmental challenges, these tools may provide valuable support between human coaching sessions or make basic coaching principles accessible to broader populations.

While these technologies offer exciting possibilities, they also raise profound questions about the essential nature of coaching. Can algorithms capture the nuanced attunement that characterises masterful coaching? Can virtual experiences generate the psychological safety required for vulnerability and growth? How do we balance technological enhancement with the fundamentally human dimensions of development?

While AI coaching has the potential to enhance and complement traditional coaching practices, there are several fundamental aspects of human coaching that AI cannot replicate. It may be worth taking a moment here to consider the limitations of the *coach-bot* and some of the key ways in which AI coaching is unlikely to ever replace human coaching.

Emotional Intelligence and Empathy

Human coaches possess emotional intelligence, allowing them to recognise and understand the feelings and emotional states of their clients. This ability to empathise is crucial for building trust and rapport. Human coaches can respond to emotional cues in real time, providing support that is sensitive to the client's emotional landscape, something AI struggles to interpret fully.

Complex Human Interactions

Coaching often involves complex conversations that require adaptability and spontaneity. Human coaches can navigate unexpected developments, adjust their approach on the fly and engage in meaningful dialogue. The ability to read body language, tone and subtleties in communication is a human skill that enhances the coaching relationship. Thus far, AI lacks the ability to perceive these non-verbal cues accurately.

Contextual Understanding

Human coaches can integrate various aspects of a client's life, including personal, professional and cultural contexts, into the coaching process. This holistic understanding is essential for providing relevant and impactful developmental support. Coaches draw on their own life experiences and insights, providing wisdom that AI, which lacks personal experiences, cannot offer.

Ethical Considerations and Moral Judgement

Human coaches can navigate complex ethical dilemmas, making judgements that consider values, morality and the nuances of human behaviour. AI operation is based on algorithms and may not account for ethical implications in the same way. Coaches can also foster a safe space for clients to share sensitive information, cultivating trust that is essential for effective coaching. Considering they are not human, it is somewhat ironic that AI systems may struggle with confidentiality concerns, given data privacy issues.

Creativity and Intuition

Human coaches can think creatively and intuitively, offering unique perspectives and innovative ideas that go beyond data-driven recommendations. Coaches can adapt and develop bespoke coaching methods based on their understanding of a client's unique personality and challenges, something AI is less capable of doing.

Relationship Building

The coaching relationship often extends over months or even years, requiring and earning deep trust and connection. Human coaches can nurture these relationships, providing continuity and stability that AI cannot match. Humans can provide encouragement, motivation and accountability in ways that resonate deeply with clients. This genuine human connection can inspire clients to take action and make lasting changes.

Reflection and Personal Growth

Human coaches excel in guiding clients through reflective processes that foster self-discovery and personal growth, using thoughtful questioning, active listening and appropriate challenge. Coaches can also deliver nuanced feedback that considers the individual's emotional state, readiness for change and personal history, which is vital for effective learning and growth.

Cultural Sensitivity and Adaptation

Human coaches are able to navigate cultural differences and sensitivities, adapting their approach to meet the diverse needs of clients from various backgrounds, something that AI may not fully grasp. Human coaches can assess the unique challenges faced by clients in their specific cultural and organisational contexts, providing tailored support that AI may not be able to adequately contextualise.

Crisis Management

In high-stakes or emotionally charged situations, human coaches can provide immediate support and guidance that takes into account the psychological impact on the client, something that AI is ill-equipped to do. Coaches can also help clients develop resilience and coping strategies based on a deep understanding of human psychology and personal experiences.

In summary, while AI can augment the coaching process by providing data-driven insights, personalised recommendations and scalable solutions, the human elements of empathy, intuition, creativity and relationship-building are (as yet) irreplaceable. The most effective coaching approaches will likely involve a blend of AI tools and human expertise, allowing coaches to leverage technology while maintaining the essential human connection that fosters growth and transformation.

Addressing Societal Challenges

Finally, the most significant future direction for coaching may involve its application to broader societal challenges. Climate change, social polarisation, economic transformation and other complex issues demand new leadership capacities and collective responses. Hopefully, future coaching approaches may explicitly address these challenges, helping leaders and organisations develop the cognitive complexity, emotional resilience and collaborative capabilities needed to address our most pressing and unprecedented collective challenges.

Continuing the Development Journey

At the conclusion of this book, it seems appropriate to return to where we began – with the recognition that coaching itself represents a developmental journey rather than a fixed destination. Just as the individuals and teams we coach continue to evolve, so too does the field of coaching and our individual practice within it.

The four approaches explored in this book – existential, systems psychodynamic, gestalt and cognitive – each offer valuable perspectives on human development in organisational contexts. Their integration creates possibilities for even more comprehensive, nuanced coaching that addresses the full spectrum of leadership and human challenges. However, even this integrated approach represents not an endpoint but a waypoint in coaching's continuing evolution.

For those who have accompanied me through these pages, I offer an invitation to continued exploration. The theoretical frameworks and practical approaches described here provide foundations for further development – both of coaching practice and of yourself as a practitioner. As we've seen in Chapter 16, the development of coaches themselves remains central to the field's advancement.

Whatever your role – coach, leader, HR professional or someone simply interested in human development – I hope this book has expanded your perspective on the possibilities coaching offers. The future of coaching will be shaped by practitioners and clients who bring curiosity, creativity and commitment to the developmental journey – qualities I've sought to embody in these pages and encourage in you as readers.

As of 2025, it is clear that the questions facing today's leaders have never been more complex or consequential. Coaching, at its best, doesn't offer simple answers to these questions but creates conditions where individuals and teams can develop the capacity to engage with complexity, navigate uncertainty and act with both wisdom and courage. By continuing to develop our coaching approaches, integrating diverse perspectives while remaining grounded in core developmental principles, we contribute to this essential capacity-building journey.

And the journey continues.

Bibliography

Anderson, J. R. (2020). *Cognitive coaching for executive performance: A guide to mental models in leadership*. Harvard Business Review Press.

Argyris, C. (1990). *Overcoming organizational defences: Facilitating organizational learning*. Allyn & Bacon.

Auerbach, J. E. (2018). *Cognitive coaching: A success-driven approach to executive development*. International Coach Federation Press.

Bachkirova, T., Spence, G., & Drake, D. (Eds.). (2017). *The SAGE handbook of coaching*. Sage Publications.

Beck, A. T. (1976). *Cognitive therapy and the emotional disorders*. International Universities Press.

Bion, W. R. (1961). *Experiences in groups*. Tavistock Publications.

Bluckert, P. (2018). *Gestalt coaching: Right here, right now*. Open University Press.

Brunning, H. (2006). *Executive coaching: Systems-psychodynamic perspective*. Karnac Books.

Chidiac, M. A. (2018). *Relational organisational gestalt: An emergent approach to organisational development*. Routledge.

Clarkson, P., & Cavicchia, S. (2021). *Gestalt coaching and consulting: Field theory in practice*. Routledge.

Cox, E., Bachkirova, T., & Clutterbuck, D. (Eds.). (2018). *The complete handbook of coaching* (3rd ed.). Sage Publications.

Critchley, B., & Casey, D. (2019). *The whole person for the whole organisation: Gestalt coaching in action*. Routledge.

Czander, W. M. (2012). *The psychodynamics of work and organisations: Theory and application*. Guilford Press.

De Haan, E. (2021). *The Tavistock tradition for leadership and organisational coaching*. Routledge.

Diamond, J. (2020). *Existential coaching skills: The handbook for practitioners*. Routledge.

Diaz, K. A. (2019). *Thinking to achieve: Cognitive coaching in leadership development*. Harvard Business Review Press.

Eisold, K. (2012). *Psychoanalytic perspectives on organisational consulting: The unconscious side of organisational life*. Lexington Books.

Ellison, J., & Hayes, C. (2020). *Cognitive coaching: Developing self-directed leaders and learners* (4th ed.). Rowman & Littlefield.

Ellis, A. (1962). *Reason and emotion in psychotherapy*. Lyle Stuart.

Frankl, V. E. (2006). *Man's search for meaning*. Beacon Press.

Future of Work Institute. (2024). *Coaching in the digital age: Trends and implications*. MIT Press.

Gillie, M., & Shackleton, M. (2017). *Gestalt in coaching: Distinctive features*. Routledge.

Grant, A. M. (2003). The impact of life coaching on goal attainment, metacognition and mental health. *Social Behaviour and Personality, 31*(3), 253–264.

Heidegger, M. (1962). *Being and time*. Harper & Row.

Huffington, C., Armstrong, D., Halton, W., Hoyle, L., & Pooley, J. (Eds.). (2018). *Working below the surface: The emotional life of contemporary organisations*. Routledge.

Ives, Y., & Cox, E. (2016). *Cognitive behavioural coaching in practice: An evidence-based approach*. Routledge.

Kegan, R. (1994). *In over our heads: The mental demands of modern life*. Harvard University Press.

Kets de Vries, M. F. R. (2014). *Mindful leadership coaching: Journeys into the interior*. Palgrave Macmillan.

Kierkegaard, S. (1992). *Either/or: A fragment of life*. Penguin Classics.

Krum, A. K. (2018). *The existential leader: An authentic approach to leadership for challenging times*. Routledge.

Langdridge, D. (2013). *Existential counselling and psychotherapy*. Sage Publications.

Latner, J., & Fodor, I. (2018). *Gestalt coaching for awareness and presence: The gestalt approach to leadership development*. Gestalt Institute Press.

Long, S. (Ed.). (2013). *Socioanalytic methods: Discovering the hidden in organisations and social systems*. Routledge.

May, R. (1983). *The discovery of being: Writings in existential psychology*. W. W. Norton.

McKenna, D. D., & Davis, S. L. (2019). *Cognitive coaching for leadership development: An evidence-based approach*. American Psychological Association.

McMahon, G. (2017). Cognitive behavioural approach to coaching. In T. Bachkirova, G. Spence, & D. Drake (Eds.), *The SAGE handbook of coaching* (pp. 258–270). Sage Publications.

Nanda, J. (2019). *Mindful existential coaching: A holistic approach to executive development*. Palgrave Macmillan.

Neenan, M., & Palmer, S. (2021). *Cognitive behavioural coaching in practice: An evidence-based approach* (2nd ed.). Routledge.

Nevis, E. C. (2013). *Organisational consulting: A Gestalt approach*. GestaltPress.

Obholzer, A., & Roberts, V. Z. (Eds.). (2019). *The unconscious at work: A Tavistock approach to making sense of organisational life* (2nd ed.). Routledge.

Palmer, S., & Szymanska, K. (2018). *Cognitive behavioural coaching: An integrative approach*. Routledge.

Parlette, M., & Beisser, A. (2015). *Gestalt theory and coaching: The paradoxical theory of change*. Gestalt International Press.

Passmore, J. (2015). *Excellence in coaching: The industry guide* (3rd ed.). Kogan Page.

Passmore, J., & Tee, D. (2021). *Coaching in three dimensions: Meeting the challenges of a complex world*. Routledge.

Perls, F. S. (1973). *The Gestalt approach and eye witness to therapy*. Science and Behaviour Books.

Rainey, M. A., & Hanafin, J. (2019). *Gestalt coaching methods: Field theory applications in leadership development*. International Gestalt Journal Press.

Rogers, C. R. (1961). *On becoming a person: A therapist's view of psychotherapy*. Houghton Mifflin.

Sartre, J.-P. (2007). *Existentialism is a humanism*. Yale University Press.

Sher, M. (2013). *The dynamics of change: Tavistock approaches to improving social systems*. Routledge.

Spinelli, E. (2014). *Being in the world: Existential perspectives on coaching*. Routledge.

Spinelli, E. (2015). Practicing existential coaching. In S. Palmer & A. Whybrow (Eds.), *Handbook of coaching psychology: A guide for practitioners* (2nd ed., pp. 198–212). Routledge.

Spoth, J., & Gold, M. (2019). *Gestalt coaching approaches for organisational contexts.* Taylor & Francis.

Stapley, L. F. (2006). *Individuals, groups, and organisations beneath the surface: An introduction.* Routledge.

Stevenson, H. (2019). *Gestalt coaching: Developing human potential in organisations.* Routledge.

Van Deurzen, E. (2012). *Existential counselling & psychotherapy in practice* (3rd ed.). Sage Publications.

Van Deurzen, E., & Hanaway, M. (Eds.). (2018). *Existential perspectives on coaching.* Palgrave Macmillan.

Williams, H., & Palmer, S. (2020). *Coaching with cognitive behavioural therapy: Evidence-based approaches for coaches.* Sage Publications.

Wolfert, R., & Sills, C. (2018). *Gestalt approaches to coaching: Working with contact boundaries.* Sage Publications.

Yalom, I. D. (2020). *Existential psychotherapy* (2nd ed.). Basic Books.

Index

For Product Safety Concerns and Information please contact our EU
representative GPSR@taylorandfrancis.com
Taylor & Francis Verlag GmbH, Kaufingerstraße 24, 80331 München, Germany